WRITING SKILLS

B a d e n
EUNSON

JOHN WILEY & SONS
BRISBANE • NEW YORK • CHICHESTER • TORONTO • SINGAPORE

First published 1994 by
JOHN WILEY & SONS
33 Park Road, Milton, Qld 4064

Offices also in Sydney and Melbourne

Typeset in 11.5/14 pt Garamond

National Library of Australia
Cataloguing-in-Publication data

Eunson, Baden.
  Writing skills.

  Bibliography.
  ISBN 0 471 33561 4.

  1. English language — Rhetoric. 2. English language —
  Grammar. I. Title. (Series: Communication skills
  (Milton, Qld.)).

808.042

Edited by Bookmark Co. Pty Ltd
All illustrations by Mike Spoor

Printed and bound in Australia by
Australian Print Group, Maryborough, Vic.

10 9 8 7 6 5 4 3 2 1

CONTENTS

• • • • • • • • •

PREFACE

. . . .

This book is for those who need to brush up on their writing skills — and it is also for those who don't have many skills to brush up on in the first place. It will prove of particular use to those who need to write basic workplace documents — letters, memos and short reports — in the course of a current or future job.

Writing Skills places such documents in the context of the mechanics of English — grammar, spelling, punctuation, vocabulary and usage. Keep in mind that some people have quite a poor grasp of mechanics, and yet write reasonably well; in contrast, others have a good grasp of mechanics, and yet write badly, or at least without flair and imagination. These extreme situations are however, just that — extreme. Most of us can measurably improve our writing by improving our knowledge of the mechanics of language.

Although this book is an introduction to the skills of writing, it is by no means exhaustive. If you need to know more about clarity and style in writing, or the techniques involved in writing particular types of documents, then you should consult other books in this series that deal with such aspects of writing.

Throughout this book, you will find numerous exercises to help you build your skills. More information about specific points in the text is contained in numbered endnotes at the back of the book. If you wish to read still further, a large and up-to-date reference list is also provided.

Baden Eunson

1

LEARNING HOW TO WRITE BETTER

Knowing how to write well is important. It can make you a better all-round communicator, and it can have real and positive pay-offs for you in your current job or in a future job. How do we learn to write well? Is such learning easy? Is it hard? Is it painful? Is it pleasant? Realistically considered, it may be all of the above. It is certainly worthwhile.

What is good writing? Perhaps you feel as though you already know, and that, therefore, this book is not for you. That may well be; but please read on a little further, just to be absolutely sure.

Consider, for example, the following items of text. What errors or ambiguities can you detect in them?

TALKING POINTS **WOULD YOU REPEAT THAT, PLEASE?**

The crocodile, estimated to be about five metres long, surfaced with open jaws just three metres from the group after it was spotted and disturbed by a rock.

Eastern Suburbs Reporter
(Fremantle, Western Australia)

Wildlife research officer Dave Berman at Alice Springs said collars had been fitted to the five females and one male after they were located using helicopters.

Tweed Daily News
(New South Wales)

Please remove your clothes when the light goes out.

Sign in laundrette

A man was fined $90 for speeding in Horsham court.

Radio news item

For your own peace of mind, have the family's electric blankets checked by a licensed electrician each year before use, especially if you have had them folded away during winter.

Instruction leaflet

We are committed to eliminating all traces of discrimination in the law against women.

US President Ronald Reagan
(speaking to the American Bar Association, 1987)

A writer remembers visiting the Dunnes fresh from Vietnam, where momentous events were expected.

Anthony Haden-Guest
Mode

One of the more interesting 'revelations' concerns the relationship that Kelly had with his mother, who after his father's death remarried an American baker about Ned's age.

Lee Tulloch
Vogue Australia

The court is hearing an appeal against the ordination of 11 women by the Anglican Bishop of Goulburn.

ABC radio news

William Buckley, the conservative editor and TV personality, is widely admired, even by such opponents as John K. Galbraith, for his mastery of the language and an ability to state propositions which are detested by the other side with grace and fluidity.

Earl Brooks and George S. Odiorne
Managing by Negotiations

The paper suggested Prince Andrew ... finally broached the subject of leaving his wife with the Queen in January this year.

Weekend Australian

Wearing plain clothes, witnesses say they saw him escape in one of the first lifeboats.

Di Webster
The Age

Unfortunately, those who do develop a taste for the RX-7 will need to be well-healed because ... the RX-7 is not the affordable fun car it was once seen as.

Royalauto

A very great wine and guilt-edged investment at the same time?

Newsletter
Farmer Bros.

No evidence linking heroine deaths.

Canberra Times

Delicious flavours of Thailand to suit any palette.

Sign outside restaurant

Slumped in his director's chair with his polo boots disguarded, Mr Packer made short work of several bottles of mineral water.

The Weekend Australian

Joeys are aged 6-8 years and are a younger version of scouts, they also wear scarves instead of uniforms.

Barossa Valley Herald

Now begin typing the correct letters, you won't be penalised for the error in your typing score — but, you will loose time; sort of a penalty anyway, so be judicious in choosing which typing errors to correct.

HELP Facility notes
TPTutor software

5 Chances of $1000 Cash

* Microwaves * Televisons * Mysery Flights *

One of these and many more could be yours

Transcontinental
Port Augusta, WA

The toilet is blocked and we cannot bath the children until it is cleared.

Would you please send someone to mend our broken path. Yesterday my wife tripped and fell on it and now she is pregnant.

Can you please tell me when our repairs are going to be done as my wife is about to become an expectant mother.

I am writing on behalf of my sink, which is running away from the wall.

Extracts from letters sent to council offices, East Yorkshire, England

Poirot, ensconced at a small table in the Blue Cat, looked up from the menu he was studying with a start . . .

Poirot inquired of the foreign young woman who opened the door for Mrs Weatherby.

Agatha Christie
Mrs McGinty's Dead

'For a person to enter those grounds and wait in prey for a number of vunerable victims to come to the toilets, then conduct the assaults is very serious and concerning.

'There is nothing to indicate he targeted one specific child. They were vunerable and he attacked them.'

Police officer investigating assaults on children
Herald Sun
(Melbourne)

People still go steady, hopefully it is the time when you fall out of romantic chemistry love and into something more lasting, intimate and friendly.

Jane Freeman
Sunday Age

BECOMING A BETTER WRITER

The weaknesses in the previous items of text are errors of grammar, punctuation, spelling and vocabulary — and, perhaps, just imprecise expression. Such weaknesses can be avoided by studying and mastering the techniques of good writing.

Knowing what and knowing why

Again, let us put the question: what is good writing? As with many things in life, people may disagree considerably about what is *good* about something, but they tend to agree more about what is *bad* about something.

If you can do anything well — writing, painting, flying, swimming — you should be able to do two things: do it well, and know why it has been done well (or know why it has not been done badly). In other words, you need to know 'why' as well as know 'what' when you write. You need to know the rules of writing, rather than just do it by 'feel', or by intuition, or creativity. Sometimes the best musicians and artists are those who have done the prolonged technical training, and then go on to express themselves creatively. They know how to best break the rules, precisely because they know the rules so well.

The rules of writing

The rules of writing involve such things as grammar, usage, punctuation, spelling and vocabulary. You can express yourself reasonably well having only a passing acquaintance with these things. You can look at various pieces of your writing and say, 'That's not bad,' or 'That's really good!' or 'That's terrible!' If you have only a passing acquaintance with the rules, however, you will be in the situation of knowing only 'what' — and not knowing 'why'.

There is also the distinct chance that you may have made some mistakes in your writing, but do not have the technical skills to recognise them as such — in other words, you may not even know 'what' as well as you might think.

To do the job properly, you've got to have the right tools.

Consider two people in a workplace. Throughout the day, they discuss a number of things — the development of their children, the problems one of them is having with her car engine, various short-cuts each has learnt about the word processing package they work with, the upcoming election. If these people can use precise terms, rather than generalities, when relating to these topics, they can communicate better and learn more. Thus the air is thick with terms such as those on the facing page.

The better informed our two people are, the better they can play out their multiple roles as parents, drivers, workers and citizens.

What if one of them had written a letter containing errors similar to the ones we have considered at the beginning of the chapter? What information would he need — what technical skills, precise vocabulary, know-how, and analytical tools and terms — to analyse and correct that letter's faults (and indeed, to ensure it had never been written that way in the first place)?

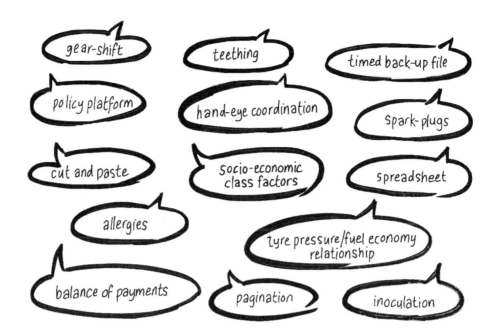

A world communicating with itself — barely

Many people crave and acquire the right verbal and conceptual tools to operate effectively in other spheres of their lives, but do not have the right tools to do the job of writing. This is a paradox, but it is a commonplace paradox: every day across the world, literally millions of letters, memos, reports, notes, faxes, electronic messages and other documents are written that just don't make sense, or are confusing, or ambiguous, or in fact convey meanings that are the very opposite of those which were intended.

This is not to mention the mis-communication that occurs daily in media articles and items, shop signs, advertisements and commercials, technical manuals, books, food and drink labels, and the thousand other artefacts of our civilisation. It is also not to mention our world of spoken communication: the way we speak and verbalise concepts — logically/illogically, elegantly/clumsily, clearly/ambiguously — is greatly affected by the level of our skill in written communication. To make our communication more effective, we need to equip ourselves with the right tools, and the right tools in this instance are those of grammar, usage, spelling, punctuation and vocabulary.

Grammar, usage, spelling, punctuation, vocabulary: why should you bother?

As the twentieth century draws to a close, and the twenty-first century looms, some people find it rather old-fashioned — rather nineteenth-century, in fact — to be concerned with these more mechanical aspects of writing. In contrast, others see these skills as timeless, and loudly lament that 'they just don't seem to teach them grammar these days'.

The reduced emphasis upon the teaching of mechanical skills in English in the past few decades has been, to a certain extent, under-standable: traditional methods of teaching were often boring, and some of the rules laid down had little relevance for the day-to-day communication tasks of real people in real situations.

The pendulum of ideas seems to be swinging back, however, to the view that a firm grasp of the fundamentals of English expression is a powerful tool, and indeed a birthright. Being skilled in these fundamentals can help you in at least two ways: it can help to minimise communication breakdowns between yourself and others, and it can help you in your career.

Death to ambiguity: minimising communication breakdowns

Communication can break down for any number of reasons: you may misinterpret my motives, I may mis-read your body language, they may perceive that the silence between the two of us shows hostility rather than empathy. Communication can also break down when we write to each other. It may well be, however, that it is easier to prevent such breakdowns when we write than when we communicate in other ways: in the world of writing, for example, the rules of communication are more clear-cut, and we can have more time to think about, and thus have more control over, what we are communicating.

Precise expression: a career-enhancing tool

In your current job, or in a future one, you may know what you want to say, but can you say it? Can you put it into words, and can you get those words down on paper? When you get your ideas onto paper, and other people read your ideas, what is their reaction? Are they impressed? Or are they less than impressed? Their reaction is, invariably, to two things, not one: the content, or the ideas, in your writing, and the process, or vehicle, for those ideas — the grammar, spelling, punctuation, vocabulary and usage. People often judge the former — what you say — by the latter — the way you say it.

'Yes, the ideas were OK, I suppose - but did you see the spelling? And the grammar, and the punctuation...? I mean, how can you take such a person seriously?'

Such judgements are sometimes unfair, picky and offensive; sometimes, however, they are fair, or at least need to be considered. They need to be considered because many people believe that if you show you have a good grasp of the fundamentals of expression, then you are also showing other things, such as the points described in table 1.1. People may be wrong in inferring such things, but they are more often right than wrong.

Table 1.1: Character traits evidenced by good written expression

Self-discipline	Grammar and related skills are not easy to acquire; this person has shown that he can knuckle down to a demanding task and succeed.
Precision and subtlety	This person has shown that she is capable of handling different types and shades of meaning; for her, language is a precision tool, rather than a blunt instrument.
Creativity	While slavish devotion to mechanical rules of expression can kill creativity, a balanced approach can produce the opposite outcome: rules of expression, once grasped, may not only act as a passive vehicle for ideas, but may help to produce better ideas — ideas with fewer ambiguities and loose ends, and more clearly-defined cause-and-effect patterns. This person is likely to have such creativity.
Personality, style, commitment	This person does not hide in a cloud of impersonality and vagueness: we receive clear and authentic messages about his identity and beliefs.
Reliability, authority, employability	This person can be counted on to make our organisation look good in our communications with our customers, and can, in fact, become one of our chief communicators. She can also become an authority within our organisation on the rights and wrongs of expression, deferred to by others. Such people are assets. If we haven't hired this person, hire her now; if we have this person on our payroll, hang on to her.

Keep in mind, also, that understanding the mechanics of language can serve your own interests even more directly: the skills of expression are also the skills of argument and persuasion, and the more persuasive you can be in communicating your ideas, the more successful you will be in being empowered to put those ideas into practice.

**Grammar,
spelling,
punctuation,
vocabulary,
usage —
they're not
pushovers.**

If you don't know already, you need to know right now: this stuff isn't easy. Learning the mechanics of English expression is quite a rigorous task. It's not quite as hard as learning another language, but it is a similar type of task. The demands are high, but then so are the pay-offs. What you are about to learn could be of enormous benefit to your career.

Let's jump into it, starting at the beginning — with words and their functions.

2

THE EIGHT PARTS OF SPEECH

THE BUILDING BLOCKS OF EXPRESSION

To understand and acquire writing skills, let's start at the beginning.

Before we learn to organise words into meaningful patterns, we need to understand the nature of words. There are eight types, or classes, of words. These are also known as the parts of speech (see table 2.1).

Table 2.1: The parts of speech

Part of speech	Function	Example
1. Nouns	name persons, places, things, qualities or concepts	Clinton, child, Jerusalem, plateau, bicycle, sadness, freedom
2. Verbs	express action or being	fly, transmit, be, appear
3. Pronouns	substitute for nouns and function as nouns	I, me, myself, mine
4. Adjectives	describe or qualify[1] or modify nouns or pronouns	tall, angry, first
5. Adverbs	modify verbs, adjectives, other adverbs or groups of words	quickly, here, soon
6. Prepositions	show relationships between a noun or pronoun and other words in a sentence	across, on, during
7. Conjunctions	link words and groups of words	and, but, because
8. Interjections	express feelings or attitudes	Wow! Hey! I say!

Don't let these terms for the parts of speech worry or confuse you. They are just names of the building blocks of expression. Before too long, you will be using the names with ease.

These eight categories are not mutually exclusive: words can appear in different categories or classes. For example, consider these groups of sentences:

1. (a) *Round* the figures off to the nearest dollar.
   (b) It's your turn to buy a *round* of drinks.
   (c) Gather *round*, everyone.
   (d) I prefer a *round* table.
   (e) This is a plant that grows the year *round*.

2. (a) I chose *that* card, not this one.
   (b) The fish *that* survived was a piranha.
   (c) Is it really *that* difficult?
   (d) I thought *that* you weren't coming.

3. (a) He walked to freedom *over* the border.
   (b) Move *over* towards me.
   (c) 'The game is *over*!' she snapped.
   (d) The cricketers had only played three of the six balls in that *over*.
   (e) 'Our radar has gone, New York. What do you advise? *Over.*'
   (f) Horse and rider *overed* the stile with ease.

4. (a) They ran outside, *but* the bus had gone.
   (b) I'd be rich now, *but* for you.
   (c) The athletes were all *but* exhausted.
   (d) 'You're going!' he shouted. 'And there's no if's or *but's* about it!'

In the first group of sentences, the word 'round' appears in all five sentences, but the word performs a different function in each sentence. In 'Round the figures off to the nearest dollar', for example, 'round' is a verb, whereas in 'It's your turn to buy a round of drinks', the same word is now a noun. In the remaining three sentences, we see 'round' appearing as an adverb, an adjective and a preposition. We see similar role changes for the words 'that', 'over' and 'but' in the other three groups of sentences. All these changes are shown in table 2.2.

The key thing to remember, then, is that **the part of speech of a word in a sentence is determined by the function of that word in that sentence.**

Table 2.2: Parts-of-speech analysis of some words

Word	Sentence	Noun	Pronoun	Verb	Adjective	Adverb	Preposition	Conjunction	Interjection
ROUND	*Round* the figures off to the nearest dollar.			■					
	It's your turn to buy a *round* of drinks.	■							
	Gather *round*, everyone.					■			
	I prefer a *round* table.				■				
	This is a plant that grows the year *round.*					■			
THAT	I chose *that* card, not this one.				■				
	The fish *that* died was a piranha.		■						
	Is it really *that* difficult?					■			
	I thought *that* you weren't coming.							■	
OVER	He walked to freedom *over* the border.						■		
	Move *over* towards me.					■			
	'The game is *over*!' she snapped.				■				
	The cricketers had only played three of the six balls in the *over.*	■							
	'Our radar is gone, New York. What do you advise? *Over.*'								■
	Horse and rider *overed* the stile with ease.*			■					
BUT	They ran outside, *but* the bus had gone.							■	
	I'd be rich now, *but* for you.						■		
	The athletes were all *but* exhausted.					■			
	'You're going!' he shouted. 'And there's no if's or *but's* about it!'	■							

* Specific North American general and sporting term

You may care to try your hand at analysing words and sentences in this manner. If so, attempt exercise 2.1 now.

You may feel, however, that you would like to get a better grip of the parts of speech before juggling with them. That's quite understandable. Let's now look at the parts of speech in greater detail, and you may choose to return to exercise 2.1 at a later time — for example, after you have completed the chapter on spelling (pp. 139), where you will see how the parts of speech can be analysed using a dictionary.

EXERCISE 2.1:

THE PARTS OF SPEECH

You may need to make multiple copies of table 2.3 for this exercise.

PART A

Analyse the following sentences by filling in the appropriate cells in table 2.3. If you are unsure of a particular part of speech for a key word, look up the word in question in a dictionary. If possible, try more than one dictionary. You may find that different dictionaries disagree on certain definitions. Dictionaries, however, do not disagree: people who write dictionaries disagree. Don't despair at this, however. See such disagreement as an opportunity for you to explore the definitions of the parts of speech. What is the essence of a noun? What function should a verb really perform? And so on.

1. Key word: BACK

(a) I think I've hurt my *back*.

(b) Every time you *back* a horse, you seem to lose money.

(c) She escaped by the *back* door.

(d) We walked *back* to the scene of the accident.

2. Key word: TILL

(a They still *till* the soil with horse-drawn ploughs.

(b) '*Till* Tuesday, then,' they said to each other as they departed.

(c) All the money had been taken from the *till*.

PART B

Discover as many meanings/parts of speech as possible for the following words. Construct sentences showing these meanings, and then analyse them, using table 2.3.

there	right	ill
so	mine	proof
okay	hail	all

Suggested answers pp. 161–62.

Table 2.3: Analysing the parts of speech

Word	Sentence	Noun	Pronoun	Verb	Adjec-tive	Adverb	Prep-osition	Conjunc-tion	Interjec-tion

NOUNS

Nouns give names to persons, places, things, qualities or concepts. They can be organised under different headings or types, as shown in table 2.4 (although many nouns might be meaningfully categorised under more than one heading). While nouns are the simplest part of speech, we need to know various things about them, such as:

- how to spell nouns (For example, is a capital letter needed?) (See p. 120.)
- how to distinguish singular and plural status (Is there one person, place, thing, quality or concept or more than one?) (See p. 131.)
- how to ensure that verbs, adjectives and pronouns agree with, or are consistent with, related nouns. (See pp. 78–83.)
- how to determine if words like 'a', 'an' or 'the' are needed before nouns.[2]

Table 2.4: Types of nouns[3]

Type of noun	What it names	Example	Characteristics
COMMON	general classes of persons, places, things, qualities, concepts	man, woman, couple, president, pope, major/officer, god, prophet, country, island, city, mountain, park, hotel, religion, day, month, festival, organisation, mother, uncle, freedom, magazine, language, nationality, computer, appliance, airline, car, tissue, ship, zeppelin, satellite, dog, monster, bird	• include all nouns except proper nouns
PROPER	• persons — by name — by title — addressed as • divine/sacred entities	Maria, John, Mr and Mrs Smith, President Clinton, Pope John Paul the President, the Pope Mr President, Your Holiness God, Yahweh, the Prophet	• sometimes reference is indirect, to show respect • *the* suggests multiplicity of identity and/or uniqueness (singular with *a/an* unlikely)
	• geographical places	Australia, Hawaii, the Kurile Islands, America/the United States, Seattle, the Hague, Mount Fujiyama, the Matterhorn, Bourbon Street, the Himalayas, Central Park, Raffles (hotel, Singapore), the Hilton (hotel)	
	• religions • days, months, festivals • organisations • family members	Christianity, Islam, Shintoism Monday, March, Christmas Rotary International, the Mafia Mother, Uncle	• when used as name, person addressed, rather than role
	• common nouns when personified and given unique reference	Freedom, Heaven, Destiny	

Type of noun	What it names	Example	Characteristics
PROPER (*continued*)	• publications	*Newsweek*, the *Sydney Morning Herald*	
	• languages	English, Russian	
	• nationalities	English, Russian, the English, Russians	
	• proprietary/brand objects	IBM, Apple, Sanyo, Aeroflot, Hyundai, Kleenex	• may also be organisations
	• objects, artefacts with specific names	*Titanic*, *Hindenberg*, *Voyager*, HAL	
	• animals given specific names	Spot, Godzilla, Tweetie	
CONCRETE	tangible things, people as individuals	rock, water, string, girl	• not often used as a category
ABSTRACT	qualities or states of being	happiness, honour, bravery	• tend to be human experiences
COUNT	• many concrete things, people as individuals	rock, string, girl, brick, mortar (weapon)	• singular and plural distinguishable; plurals usually indicated by adding -*s* or -*es* to singular form
	• units of measurement	hour, peso, kilometre	
	• individual parts of a mass	bit, remnant, sliver	• quantitative variation described by *fewer*, *many:* fewer bricks
	• many abstract nouns (countable)	triumph, opinion, mind, decision	
MASS	• many abstract things	happiness, serenity, permanence	• do not usually form plurals
	• substances, gases	earth, (pile of) string, milk, water, mortar, ozone, money	• quantitative variation described by *less*, *much:* less mortar
	• many verbal nouns (gerunds) (see p. 36)	running, teaching, stretching	
	• most diseases	AIDS, cholera	
COLLECTIVE	groups of people, animals, things	committee, team, public, class, flock, pride, gaggle, fleet	• can be thought of as singular or plural, depending upon whether emphasis is upon group as a whole or upon members of group

VERBS

Verbs are words that express action or being. There's a lot we need to know about verbs, but not necessarily here and now: thus we will defer until next chapter a detailed exploration of mysteries such as tense, transitivity, mood, voice and variations in form.

The key thing to note about verbs here is how they play a part in forming sentences. Verbs work with nouns (and pronouns: see p. 16) to form the basic structure of all sentences. Consider for example these basic sentences:

> Birds fly.
> John laughs.
> The water evaporated.

Apart from *the* in the second sentence, both sentences can be seen as simple noun + verb constructions:

Noun	Verb
birds	fly
John	laughs
water	evaporated

These sentences are making simple statements about people or things, telling us what happened. When something or someone flies, laughs or evaporates, action occurs. Not surprisingly, these verbs are known as *action verbs*.

The other major types of verb we need to know about at this stage are those which do not show action but those which show being or appearance, such as 'be', 'seem', 'is', 'were', 'appear', 'becomes'. These are known as *being verbs*.[4]

Verbs and nouns (and pronouns) make up the key parts of the two sections of most sentences. These two sections are known as the subject and the predicate.

Subject	Predicate
The man	left.
Maria	sent a fax.
Happiness	fades quickly.
Mrs Smith	is annoyed by the delays.
The enormous ship	disappeared beneath the waves.
The dilapidated computer screen	slowly revealed the entire spreadsheet.

Note that:

- The SUBJECT of a sentence names the person, place, thing, quality or concept about which something is being said — that is, what the sentence is about.
- The PREDICATE of a sentence says something about the person, place, thing, quality or concept named in the subject.
- A COMPLETE SENTENCE requires both a subject and a predicate.
- The key part of a subject is a NOUN (or pronoun).
- The key part of a predicate is a VERB.

We will soon expand this last definition to read 'the key part of a predicate is a *finite* verb' (p. 32), but the shorter definition will do for now. We will also soon see how modifiers such as adjectives and adverbs can add to the meaning of nouns (and pronouns) and verbs. However, the key aspect of sentence structure exists in the meanings given by nouns, pronouns and verbs. If adverbs and adjectives — for example, *enormous, dilapidated, slowly* — were removed from the previous examples of sentences, their meanings would still remain. If, however, nouns or verbs — for example, *ship, disappeared, computer, revealed* — were removed, the sentences would become meaningless.

PRONOUNS

Pronouns can substitute for nouns or function in a noun-like way. For example:

> Maria handed the portable computer to John, and said that she was unhappy with the way it had been running.

In this sentence, there are two pronouns: *she* and *it*. *She* is the pronoun standing in the place of the noun, *Maria*, while the noun, *Maria*, is known as the *antecedent* of the pronoun *she*. Similarly, *it* is the pronoun standing in the place of the noun, *computer*, and the noun, *computer*, is known as the antecedent of the pronoun, *it*.

There are eight major types of pronoun (see table 2.5).

Table 2.5: Types of pronouns

Type of pronoun	Function	Examples	Examples in sentences
PERSONAL	refers to persons or things	I, me, mine, you, she, her, them, it, ours	*I* think that *you* should go with *them*.
RELATIVE	relates groups of words to nouns or to other pronouns (see noun clauses and adjective clauses, p. 56)	that, what, who, whom, whoever, which	She loaded the software *that* was defective.
INDEFINITE	do not actually substitute for nouns, but function as nouns: refer to non-specific persons or things	anybody, everybody, all, some, each, one, none	*Anybody* could get a job there.
DEMONSTRATIVE	identifies or points to nouns	this, that, these, those, such	*That* was the faulty terminal.
INTERROGATIVE	introduces questions	that, whose, which, who	*Who* is there?
INTENSIVE	intensifies antecedent	himself, myself, themselves	I, *myself*, will choose the furniture.
REFLEXIVE	similar to intensive, except that sentence subject also receives action of verb	himself, myself, themselves	He compromised *himself*.
RECIPROCAL	refers to individual parts of a plural antecedent	each other, one another	Maria and Jane like *each other*.

Notice that some types of pronouns can appear in more than one category of pronoun. As we have seen in considering the more general concepts of the parts of speech, the meaning of a word is determined by the function it performs in a sentence.

Notice also the pronoun groups I/me/mine, she/her and who/whom. Why is there a difference? When do you use one, and not the other(s)? The differences within these pronoun groups relate to a property of some pronouns and all nouns called *case*, and this relates to whether the word in question is part of the sentence subject or part of the sentence predicate, or to whether ownership or possession needs to be shown. We will look at *case* in detail on p. 66.

EXERCISE 2.2:

SUBJECT AND PREDICATE

Locate the subject and predicate of each of the following sentences.

Example:

Subject	Predicate
The photocopier	seems to be malfunctioning.

(a) The chair squeaks.
(b) The report was late.
(c) Christmas seems a long way away.
(d) Both printers — the laser jet and the bubble jet — kept jamming.
(e) A complete warehouse-full of printers may need to be checked.

Answers on p. 163.

• •

EXERCISE 2.3:

NOUNS, PRONOUNS AND VERBS

Locate nouns, pronouns and verbs in the following sentences.

Example:

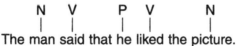

The man said that he liked the picture.

(a) The printer hummed.
(b) Those were the printers which had problems.
(c) We rarely experience problems like that.
(d) The mechanic also said that he, himself, had little experience with similar faults.
(e) Get him to look at yours and mine before he goes.

Answers on p. 163.

• •

ADJECTIVES AND ADVERBS: THE MAJOR MODIFIERS

We know that the same word can function as different parts of speech. In Exercise 2.3 above, consider the word *experience* in previous sentences (c) and (d). In sentence (c), *experience* is a verb — a doing word. In sentence (d), *experience* is a noun — a naming word. The meaning of both words in their respective sentences is changed or modified slightly by the words in front of them — *rarely* in sentence (c), and *little* in sentence (d). *Rarely* is an adverb, modifying the meaning of the verb *experience*, while *little* is an adjective, modifying the meaning of the noun, *experience*.

Adverbs and adjectives modify the meaning of other words. They tell us more about other words, adding to or subtracting from the base or root meaning of those other words. Other parts of speech, such as nouns and verb forms, can also modify nouns, as in the following constructions:

Noun modifying noun	Verb form modifying noun
instruction manual	running water
summer breeze	defeated enemy
postage stamp	frozen juice

However, let's concentrate here on the major modifiers — adjectives and adverbs — and defer detailed analysis of other modifiers until later (nouns: p. 88; verbal forms: p. 33).

Adjectives

Adjectives modify nouns and pronouns. What do adjectives tell us? They answer the questions

- What kind?
- Which one?
- How many?
- Whose?

Thus, typical adjectives would be *blue* tie, *seventh* day, *three* windows, *his* letter.[5] Strictly speaking, the words *a*, *an* and *the* are also adjectives, because they modify nouns. *The* is known as the definite article, while *a/an* is referred to as the indefinite article. (The article *an* tends to be used with words beginning with vowels [*a, e, i, o, u*]; the article *a* tends to be used with words beginning with consonants [*b, c, d, f* ...].)

Sometimes it is easy to confuse adjectives with pronouns. The same word can function as either an adjective or a pronoun — it simply depends upon the function it is playing in a sentence. Consider the following examples:

Adjectives	Pronouns
Her hair is long.	Jane won, but I still don't like *her*.
Some people prefer it like that.	I like *some*, but not others.
These screens are flickering too much.	I think *these* are better.
Each person can make their own choice.	Give one drink to *each*.

Adverbs

Adverbs modify verbs, adjectives, other adverbs and groups of words. What do adverbs tell us? They answer the questions:

- Where?
- When?
- How?
- How often?
- To what extent or degree?

Thus, typical adverbs might be died *there*, *quite* late, *completely* through, as *regularly* as clockwork, *entirely* up to them.

Adverbs are often distinguishable by their *-ly* suffixes or endings. Some adverbs, however — *forever*, *around* — are quite unlike this. Note that some adjectives also have *-ly* endings — *early*, *lively*, *ghastly* — and this might lead to confusion. It may irritate some readers and listeners if you try to use such adjectives adverbially (*early abandoned*) or try to convert adjectives to adverbs by giving them a double suffix (*ghastlily*)[6]. In such cases, it may be better to entirely recast or restructure your sentence.

We will look at adjectives and adverbs in greater detail in chapter 8 (p. 84). In the meantime, try the following exercise, which may help to clarify the roles of adjectives, adverbs, nouns and verbs.

EXERCISE 2.4:

NOUNS, VERBS, ADJECTIVES AND ADVERBS

(a) Complete table 2.6, filling in other parts of speech for each word. The first sequence (laughter/laugh/laughable/laughably) is given as an example. If there is no part of speech for a base word, then that cell of the table has been shaded in.

Table 2.6: Word changes by parts of speech

Noun	Verb	Adjective	Adverb
laughter/laugh	laugh	laughable	laughably
progress		progressive	
	approve		
		hopeful	
		happy	
		tabular	
			reliably
love			
	suspect		
			attractively
irritation			
	separate		

Answers on p. 164.

(b) Construct sentences showing appropriate usage of each of the 48 words in the table. Try to use more than one part of speech for a given word in one sentence — use the noun and adverb forms of one word in one sentence, the noun/verb/adjective/adverb forms of a word in another sentence. For example:

> When you hear her *laugh* in person, you will realise how *laughably* absurd it is to think that it is her voice on the tape — a proposition as *laughable* as the rest of the prosecution's case.

PREPOSITIONS

Prepositions are words that combine with nouns or pronouns (and any attached modifiers) to form phrases. (Some examples of common and compound prepositions are listed below.) These phrases are groups of words that modify other words. Prepositional phrases acting as adjectives modify nouns and pronouns, while prepositional phrases acting as adverbs modify verbs, adjectives, other adverbs, or groups of words.

For example, look at the following sentence.

I walked through the gates of the city.

Through the gates is an adverbial prepositional phrase modifying the verb *walked* (answering the adverbial question 'Where?'), whereas *of the city* is an adjectival prepositional phrase modifying the noun *gates* (answering the adjectival question 'Which ones?').

Common prepositions

about	below	for	out	under
above	beneath	from	outside	underneath
across	beside	in	over	unlike
after	between	inside	past	until
against	beyond	into	regarding	up
along	but	like	round	upon
among	by	near	since	with
around	concerning	next	through	within
as	despite	of	throughout	without
at	down	off	till	
before	during	on	to	
behind	except	onto	toward	

Compound prepositions

according to	in addition to	next to
along with	in accordance with	on account of
apart from	in case of	on top of
because of	in favour of	out of
by means of	in front of	regardless of
contrary to	in place of	with regard to
due to	in spite of	with the exception of
except for	instead of	

EXERCISE 2.5:

PREPOSITIONAL PHRASES

Identify the prepositional phrases in the following memo. Underline the phrase, write what type of phrase it is above it, and draw an arrow from the phrase to the word it modifies. For example:

```
           adverbial       adjectival
         ┌──────────────┐ ┌──────────┐
I walked through the gates of the city.
```

CLONE POWER

Site 39, Rintrah Industrial Park, Claymore 23121 Freedonia

Telephone (61.5) 233.4352 • Facsimile (61.5) 233.4378

MEMORANDUM

To: John Alden
From: Priscilla Khan
Subject: Juggernaut Manufacturing
Date: July 6, 1994

Juggernaut may give us a large contract within two weeks. Our rep in that area feels that they will buy equipment from us, despite the recession. Please contact the manager of Juggernaut's computer maintenance department without delay and assure him/her of our reliability.

I want this account to be given high priority in the new financial year. Sales performance in this area has been extremely good, and I think everyone in the company should know about it before the week is done.

Answers on page 165.

CONJUNCTIONS

Conjunctions are words that link other words or groups of words. The most common conjunctions are *and* and *but* — for example:

The dog *and* the cat were fighting.
The project was completed over budget *but* within time.

In the first sentence, the conjunction *and* links nouns and adjectives/ definite articles, while in the second sentence the conjunction *but* links adverbial prepositional phrases.

Correlative conjunctions work in pairs: both ... and, neither ... nor, not only ... but also, either ... or, whether ... or, as ... as.

> *Both* the report *and* the memo were available, but *neither* Maria *nor* John had seen them.

We will return to conjunctions at a later stage when we are considering groups of words known as clauses (p. 54).

INTERJECTIONS

Interjections are words that are thrown into a sentence to express surprise or some other strong emotion. They are punctuated with an exclamation mark if they are strongly emphatic; otherwise, they are usually followed by a comma or dash:

> Hey!   God, what a mess.   Mmmm, I thought so.   What a pity — it's broken.

Interjections have no grammatical function; they are not a part of the subject or predicate of a sentence.

EXERCISE 2.6:

PARTS OF SPEECH — OVERVIEW

Identify the parts of speech of the underlined words in the following memo. Record the different words in table 2.7.

Answers on p. 166.

CLONE POWER

Site 39, Rintrah Industrial Park, Claymore 23121 Freedonia

Telephone (61.5) 233.4352 • Facsimile (61.5) 233.4378

MEMORANDUM

To: Roberta and Brian
From: John A.
Subject: The networking report
Date: 4/4/94

When <u>this report</u> was <u>finally</u> printed out, it <u>was a mess</u>. The charts were printed <u>not only in</u> the <u>wrong</u> colours <u>but also on the</u> wrong pages. I need this <u>quite early</u> tomorrow, and I want the problem fixed <u>quickly</u>. <u>Really</u>, I'm not pleased with <u>this</u> situation. <u>Either</u> we <u>fix this now</u>, <u>or first</u> thing tomorrow morning. <u>Either</u> course is unpalatable. Choose <u>either</u>.

Table 2.7: Parts of speech analysis

Nouns	Verbs	Pronouns	Adjectives

Adverbs	Prepositions	Conjunctions	Interjections

· ·

VERBS: THE FULL STORY

We have briefly looked at verbs already in chapter 2. We learnt that verbs:
- express action or being
- form the basis of sentences, together with nouns and pronouns
- form the key part of the predicate of a sentence.

In this chapter, we will learn much more about this basic building block of writing. We will look at:
- transitive and intransitive verbs
- linking and auxiliary verbs
- finite and non-finite verbs
- number and person of verbs
- tense of verbs
- voice and mood of verbs.

TRANSITIVE AND INTRANSITIVE VERBS

Let's look at a dictionary entry for a simple word — 'read'.

read¹ /rid/, *v.*, **read** /rɛd/, **reading** /ˈridɪŋ/, *n.* –*v.t.* **1.** to observe, and apprehend the meaning of (something written, printed, etc.): *to read a book.* **2.** to utter aloud; render in speech (something written, printed, etc.). **3.** to have such knowledge of (a language) as to be able to understand things written in it: *to be able to read French.* **4.** to apprehend the meaning of (signs, characters, etc.) otherwise than with the eyes, as by means of the fingers. **5.** to make out the significance of, by scrutiny or observation: *to read the sky.* **6.** to foresee, foretell, or predict: *to read a person's fortune.* **7.** to make out the character, etc., of (a person, etc.), as by the interpretation of outward signs. **8.** to understand or take (something read or observed) in a particular way. **9.** to introduce (something not expressed or directly indicated) into what is read or considered. **10.** to adopt or give as a reading in a particular passage: *for 'one thousand' another version reads 'ten thousand'.* **11.** to register or indicate, as a thermometer or other instrument. **12.** (of a computer) to take (information) from a peripheral device, as a set of punched cards, into the central computer. **13.** to study, as by perusing books: *to read law.* **14.** to learn by, or as if by, perusal: *to read a person's thoughts.* **15.** to bring, put, etc., by reading: *to read oneself to sleep.* **16.** to give one (a lecture or lesson) by way of admonition or rebuke. **17.** to discover or explain the meaning of (a riddle, a dream, etc.). **18.** (of a computer) to copy (information) from a secondary device, such as a magnetic tape or disc, into its primary storage area. –*v.i.* **19.** to read or peruse writing, printing, etc., or papers, books, etc. **20.** to utter aloud, or render in speech, written or printed words that one is perusing: *to read to a person.* **21.** to give a public reading or recital. **22.** to inspect and apprehend the meaning of written or other signs or characters. **23.** to occupy oneself seriously with reading or study, esp. in a specific course of study: *to read for holy orders.* **24.** to obtain knowledge or learn of something by reading. **25.** to admit of being read, esp. properly or well. **26.** to have a certain wording. **27.** to admit of being read or interpreted (as stated): *a rule that reads two different ways.* **28.** (of a computer) to take in information. **29. read between the lines**, to perceive the truth of a situation, regardless of its appearances. **30. read oneself in**, *C. of E.* to take possession of a benefice by publicly reading the Thirty-nine Articles. **31. you wouldn't read about it!** (an exclamation of astonishment, sometimes ironic). –*n.* **32.** the act or process of reading: *I just lay in bed and had a good read.* **33. a good read**, a book, magazine, etc., that is enjoyable to read. [ME *rede* (*n*), OE *rædan* counsel, consider, read, c. D *raden*, G *raten*, Icel. *radha*]

Figure 3.1: The word *read*

(Source: *The Macquarie Dictionary* (1991:1466) Second Edition. North Ryde: Macquarie Library Pty Ltd) Reproduced with permission.

It looks complicated, but it's not. Notice that the entry is broken up into multiple meanings of the word.[7] Meanings 1-18 are preceded by the abbreviation *v.t.*, while meanings 19-31 are preceded by the abbreviation *v.i.* The term *v.t.* means transitive verb, and the term *v.i.* means intransitive verb. Some other dictionaries will use the terms *tr.* (transitive verb) and *intr.* (intransitive verb). Whichever naming system is used, reference is being made to different applications of the same base verb. Here's an example of those different applications:

Transitive	Intransitive
I read books.	I read.

Notice that the transitive form is connected to another word, the noun *books*.

The subject = I
The predicate = read books.

The noun *books* is also referred to as the direct object. Thus a transitive verb is one which has a direct impact upon a person or thing in the predicate.

In contrast, the intransitive form of the verb *read* does not require a direct object to complete its meaning. It makes perfect sense to simply say 'I read/I am reading/I have read/Do you read?' Thus an intransitive verb is one which has no direct impact upon a person or thing mentioned in the predicate.

The word 'transitive' comes from a Latin word meaning 'to pass over'. In other words, a transitive verb is passing over from the subject to the object — it's in transit from the subject to the object. An intransitive verb, by contrast, isn't in transit to anywhere — it doesn't need to move to, or relate to, anything else to complete its meaning.

Not all verbs have both transitive and intransitive meanings. Table 3.1 gives some examples of verbs with either a transitive or an intransitive meaning.

Table 3.1: Transitive and intransitive verbs

SUBJECT	PREDICATE	
	Transitive verb	Direct object
Indira	brings	food.
She	mortgaged	her home.
Jack	mentioned	the rumour.
Aileen	will patch	that.

SUBJECT	PREDICATE	
	Intransitive verb	
We	arrived	late.
The objects	materialised	on the table.
The objects	vanished	in a puff of smoke.
They	smirked	at her misfortunes.

Notice that with transitive verbs, action occurs upon something or someone: it is possible to engage in the acts of bringing, mortgaging, mentioning and patching something or someone. In contrast, it is not standard English to try and arrive, materialise, vanish or smirk something or someone. The test of a transitive verb is to take the action of the verb and place it in a question with *what* or *who* (see table 3.2).

Table 3.2: Examples of testing for transitive and intransitive verbs

Verb	Who/what question	Meaningful answer?	Answer	Verb type
brings	brings who/what?	yes	food	*vt*
arrived	arrived who/what?	no	—	*vi*
mortgaged	mortgaged who/what?	yes	her home	*vt*
materialised	materialised who/what?	no	—	*vi*
mentioned	mentioned who/what?	yes	rumour	*vt*
vanished	vanished who/what?	no	—	*vi*
will patch	will patch who/what?	yes	that	*vt*
smirked	smirked who/what?	no	—	*vi*

The non-verb words in the predicates of intransitive sentences answer questions like *When?* and *Where?* — they are thus modifiers, rather than direct objects.

LINKING AND AUXILIARY VERBS

We have been dealing with *action* verbs. What about *being* verbs? These are the forms of the verb to be — for example:

is   am   be   was   were   been   being   are   shall be
will be   shall have been   will have been

Being verbs, however, also include the following:

remain   seem   become   smell   grow   taste   sound   make

Being verbs cannot have a direct object — there is nothing to 'carry over' to something else. *Being* verbs also cannot form a predicate on their own — other words are required. *Being* verbs thus play the role of *linking* verbs. Such *linking* verbs (also known as *copulative* verbs) serve to rename or describe a sentence subject by linking it with a noun or adjective in the predicate. Such a noun or adjective is known as a *subject complement* (see table 3.3).

Table 3.3: Verbs and subject complements

SUBJECT	PREDICATE		Subject complement type
	Linking verb	Subject complement	
She	was	supervisor.	predicate noun
She	was	angry.	predicate adjective
The building	became	rubble.	predicate noun
The building	looked	attractive.	predicate adjective
Spot the dog	remained	the leader.	predicate noun
Spot the dog	remained	hungry.	predicate adjective

Another group of verbs, different from finite, non-finite and linking verbs, are known as *auxiliary* or *helping* verbs. These include the verb *to be*, and other verbs such as:

shall   should   will   would   can   could   do   did

may   must   might   have   has   had

These verbs work with other verbs to show variations in tense or time, and to form questions — for example:

I *should* reject their offer when it comes.
Should I reject their offer when it comes?
He *could have* gone later.
Maria *might have* only scratched it.

In such sentences, the verb being helped by the auxiliary, or helping, verb is known as the *main* verb.

TALKING POINTS

SHOULD, WOULD, SHALL, WILL ...

There is some controversy over whether it is better to use *should* or *would*, or *shall* or *will*, in certain sentences. The two sides of the controversy follow.

One point of view: S. H. Burton

The rules are:
- For first person singular and plural, use shall and should.
- For second and third person singular and plural, use will and would.
  For example:

  I *shall* stay in Paris. (first person singular)
  You *will* stay in Paris. (second person singular or plural)
  We said that we *should* take a taxi. (first person plural)
  They said that they *would* take a taxi. (third person plural)

Nowadays, there is general ignorance of the correct use of *shall/will* and *should/would*. That ignorance impairs linguistic precision. The rules should be known — and kept.

Another point of view: the *American Heritage Dictionary*

The traditional rules for using *shall* and *will* prescribe a highly complicated pattern of use in which the meanings of the forms change according to the person of the subject. In the first person, *shall* is used to indicate simple futurity: *I shall* (not *will*) *have to buy another ticket*. In the second and third persons, the same sense of futurity is expressed by will: *The comet will* (not *shall*) *return in 87 years. You will* (not *shall*) *probably encounter some heavy seas when you round the point*. The use of *will* in the first person and *shall* in the second and third may express determination, promise, obligation, or permission, depending on the context. Thus, *I will leave tomorrow* indicates that the speaker is determined to leave; *You and she shall leave tomorrow* is likely to be interpreted as a command. The sentence, *You shall have your money* expresses a promise ('I will see that you get your money'), whereas *You will have your money* makes a simple prediction.

Such, at least, are the traditional rules. But the distinction has never taken firm root outside of what H. W. Fowler described as 'the English of the English' (as opposed to that of the Scots and Irish), and even there it has always been subject to variation. Despite the efforts of generations of American schoolteachers, the distinction is largely alien to the modern American idiom. In America, *will* is used to express most of the senses reserved for *shall* in English usage, and *shall* itself is restricted to first person interrogative proposals, as in *Shall we go?* and to certain fixed expressions, such as *We shall overcome. Shall* is also used in formal style to express an explicit obligation, as in *Applicants shall provide a proof of residence*, though this sense is also expressed by *must* or *should*. In speech, the distinction that the English signal by the choice of *shall* or *will* may be rendered by stressing the auxiliary, as in *I* will *leave tomorrow* ('I intend to leave'); by choosing another auxiliary, such as *must* or *have to*; or by using an adverb, such as *certainly*.

Many early American writers observed the traditional distinction between *shall* and *will*, and some continue to do so. The practice cannot be called incorrect, though it may strike American ears as somewhat mannered. But the distinction is difficult for those who do not come by it natively, and Americans who essay a *shall* in an unfamiliar context run considerable risk of getting it wrong, and so of being caught out in that most embarrassing of linguistic gaffes, the bungled Anglicism . . .

Like the rules governing *shall* and *will* on which they are based, the traditional rules governing the use of *should* and *would* are largely ignored in modern American practice. Either *should* or *would* can now be used in the first person to express conditional futurity: *If I had known that, I would* (or somewhat more formally, *should*) *have answered differently*. But in the second and third persons, only *would* is used: *If he had known that, he would* (not *should*) *have answered differently. Would* cannot always be substituted for *should*, however. *Should* is used in all three persons in a conditional clause: *if I* (or *you* or *he*) *should go*. On the other hand, *would* is used to express volition or promise: *I agreed that I would do it.* Either *would* or *should* is possible as an auxiliary with *like, be inclined, be glad, prefer*, and related verbs: *I would* (or *should*) *like to call your attention to an oversight.*[8]

(Source: *The American Heritage Dictionary of the English Language.* Third Edition. Reprinted by permission Houghton Mifflin Company © 1992.)

EXERCISE 3.1:

TYPES OF VERBS

Identify transitive, intransitive, linking and auxiliary verbs in the following sentences. Write the abbreviations *vt, vi, vl* and *va* above the appropriate verbs.

(a) He worked all day.
(b) I can't work miracles.
(c) Shall we dance?
(d) The quick brown fox jumped over the lazy dog.
(e) The entire debate turned on the question of whether the economy had turned the corner.
(f) It sounded appalling, but I could not disconnect the machine.
(g) These photocopies still feel warm.
(h) Shouldn't we just go anyway?
(i) Automation has been a disaster at this plant.
(j) They must meet this deadline by tomorrow.

Answers on p. 166.

VERBS: NUMBER AND PERSON

Verbs change according to person and number (see table 3.4).

- The first person (singular and plural) relates to the person speaking or writing. The pronouns *I* and *we* are the only subjects that occur in the first person.
- The second person (singular and plural) relates to the person who is being spoken or written to. In modern English, the same pronoun — *you* — is used for both the singular and plural. This pronoun is the only subject that occurs in the second person.
- The third person is the person(s) or thing(s) being spoken about. Nouns and a wide variety of pronouns can be used for subjects in the third person.

Table 3.4: Verbs — number and person

		NUMBER	
		Singular	**Plural**
PERSON	**First**	I	We
	Second	You	You
	Third	He, she, it, the accountant	Them, the accountants

The concepts of number and person are quite basic, and it is hard to imagine that they could lead to confusion and ambiguity in expression. Yet, as we shall see later (p. 78, p. 93), sloppy handling of these basics can lead to mistakes in subject–verb agreement and inappropriate shifts in number and person. As we shall see now, number and person are important factors in determining just what is, and what is not, a verb.

FINITE AND NON-FINITE VERBS

Consider the following groups of words:

I type.	I speak.
I typed.	I spoke.
I have typed.	I have spoken.
typed letters	spoken commentary
having typed	having spoken
I am typing.	I was speaking.
typing speed	speaking engagement
Typing can be difficult.	Do you find speaking stressful?
To type is a real skill.	They want you to speak.

At first glance, the word groups simply appear to be variations on two basic verbs — *to type* and *to speak*. And indeed, that is what they are. But how many of the variations of *to type* and *to speak* are real verbs, and how many of them, in fact, comprise quite different parts of speech?

All of these word groups are examples of precise grammatical constructions. Let's look at their actual names in table 3.5, and learn just where the real verbs are.

Table 3.5: Finite and non-finite forms of two verbs

Simple/base form	I *type*.	I *speak*.
Past tense	I *typed*.	I *spoke*.
Past participle + auxiliary	I have *typed*.	I have *spoken*.
Past participle	*typed* letters	*spoken* commentary
Perfect participle	having *typed*	having *spoken*
Present participle + auxiliary	I am *typing*.	I was *speaking*.
Present participle	*typing* speed	*speaking* engagement
Gerund	*Typing* can be difficult.	Do you find *speaking* stressful?
Infinitive	To *type* is a real skill.	They want you to *speak*.

The simple, base, plain or dictionary forms of the verbs are *type* and *speak*. These are also known as finite verbs. This form will always be the first entry in the dictionary definition of a particular verb. Infinitive forms (*to type, to speak*) also comprise fundamental ways of defining a verb, but misunderstandings can arise when they are used as they are in our examples, where in fact they appear as nouns. Why? Read on.

The simple form is known as a finite verb because it is limited or finite in relation to subject, person, number and tense (or time) (see p. 37). This simply means that the verb changes according to the subject it is relating to:

> I type slowly.
> She types quickly.
> They type quickly.
> John spoke well.
> Maria speaks indistinctly.
> They will speak as a team.

The fact that finite verbs actually have subjects differentiates them from non-finite verbs, which do not. A finite verb is part of the predicate of a sentence or clause, and in fact can comprise a predicate simply by itself, which is known as a clause. Clauses are discussed in chapter 4 (pp. 53–56).

There are five types of non-finite verbs — *past participle*, *perfect participle*, *present participle*, *gerund* and *infinitive*.

These are called non-finite because they are not limited by subject, person, number or tense. In fact, unless they are given some help, they are not true verbs at all. Non-finite verbs can be part of the subject or predicate of a sentence or clause. Non-finite verbs, to repeat, do not have a subject.

A participle is a form of a verb that requires an auxiliary or helping verb (see p. 28) to form particular tenses and, by itself, functions as an adjective. Take, for example, the past participle.

The past participle

The past participle needs an auxiliary or helping verb to form *perfect tenses* (see p. 37) and *passive constructions* (see p. 42). The past participle of a verb looks suspiciously like the past tense of a verb: notice, for example, that '*typed* letters' uses the same form of 'type' as the past tense 'I typed'. But notice, also, that the past participle '*spoken* commentary' is different from the past tense 'I spoke'. This is because 'type' is a *regular* verb, and 'speak' is an *irregular* verb. A regular verb is simply a verb that forms its past tense and past participle by by adding -*d* or -*ed* to its plain, base, simple or dictionary form. Irregular verbs form their past tense and past participle forms in irregular ways. There are approximately 250 irregular verbs in English, and some of these are shown in table 3.6.

Table 3.6: Irregular verbs — a checklist

Simple/ base form	Past tense	Past participle
arise	arose	arisen
be (am, is, are)	was, were	been
become	became	become
begin	began	begun
bid (offer)	bid	bid
bid (command)	bade	bidden
bite	bit	bitten/bit
break	broke	broken
bring	brought	brought
buy	bought	bought
choose	chose	chosen
come	came	come
do	did	done
draw	drew	drawn
drink	drank	drunk
drive	drove	driven
eat	ate	eaten
fall	fell	fallen
find	found	found
flee	fled	fled
forgot	forgot	forgotten/forgot
forgive	forgave	forgiven
freeze	froze	frozen
get	got	got/gotten
give	gave	given
go	went	gone
grow	grew	grown
hang (suspend)	hung	hung
hang (execute)	hanged	hanged
hide	hid	hidden
know	knew	known
lay	laid	laid
lead	led	led

Simple/ base form	Past tense	Past participle
leave	left	left
let	let	let
lie	lay	lain
lose	lost	lost
make	made	made
pay	paid	paid
prove	proved	proved/proven
ride	rode	ridden
ring	rang	rung
rise	rose	risen
run	ran	run
say	said	said
see	saw	seen
seek	sought	sought
set	set	set
shake	shook	shaken
sing	sang/sung	sung
sink	sank/sunk	sunk
sit	sat	sat
slide	slid	slid
speak	spoke	spoken
spring	sprang/sprung	sprung
stand	stood	stood
steal	stole	stolen
strike	struck	struck
swim	swam	swum
tear	tore	torn
think	thought	thought
throw	threw	thrown
understand	understood	understood
wake	woke/waked	waked/woken
wear	wore	worn
write	wrote	written

The perfect participle

The perfect participle is formed by simply combining with the past participle.

> *Having typed* the letter, she went home.
> *Having spoken* her mind, she felt more at ease.

Perfect participles usually appear in longer phrases, and behave like adjectives, modifying or telling us about the sentence subject (see perfect tenses, p. 39).

The present participle

The present participle is formed by adding the suffix *-ing* to the plain or base form of the verb.

> Her *typing* speed was less than ideal.
> The *speaking* engagement was for next Friday afternoon.

The present participle functions as an adjective. It can only become a verb with the assistance of an auxiliary or helping verb and, when this occurs, it forms the progressive forms of the tenses (*was typing, am typing, will be typing,* etc.) (see progressive tenses, p. 39).

The gerund

The gerund is merely the past participle taking off its 'adjective' hat and putting on its 'noun' hat.

> *Typing* is something I don't do as well as I should.
> I find *speaking* stressful.

The infinitive

The infinitive is formed by adding *to* to the plain or base form of the verb.

> *To type* is a real skill.
> They want you *to speak*.

Remember: prepositional phrases can also begin with *to*.

> *to* the limit
> *to* the front door

A prepositional phrase will have a noun following *to*, whereas an infinitive will have a verb root following *to*.

> You will need *to limit* your workload (infinitive).
> I will work *to the limit* of my power (prepositional phrase).

EXERCISE 3.2

NON-FINITE VERBS

Underline the non-finite verbs in the following sentences, and identify them by type (past participle, perfect participle, present participle, gerund and infinitive). Circle the main verbs in the sentences.

Remember that only a finite verb can have a subject, and it forms all or part of the predicate of a sentence or clause. Non-finite verbs do not have a subject, and can form all or part of the predicate or subject of a sentence or clause.

(a) She handed the typed letters to me.
(b) Having looked over the papers, she looked out of the window.
(c) He asked me to go later.
(d) Walking through the park is my favourite activity.
(e) My walking shoes are extremely comfortable.

Answers on p. 167.

ACTION AND BEING IN TIME: VERBS AND TENSE

The tense of a verb tells us when an action or state takes place. Don't be dismayed by the terminology used in describing tenses: if you look at the categories in the table of tenses following (table 3.7), you may find the *names* of categories or types of tenses incomprehensible, but if you look at the *examples* inside the table, you will find that you are familiar with virtually all tenses and, in fact, are capable of making quite subtle discriminations in tense use. You've been using tenses all your life — so don't get tense about tense!

Table 3.7: Simple, perfect and progressive tenses of a regular verb and an irregular verb (active voice)

		REGULAR VERB: TO TYPE		IRREGULAR VERB: TO SPEAK	
		Singular	**Plural**	**Singular**	**Plural**
		SIMPLE TENSES			
PRESENT	First person	I type.	We type.	I speak.	We speak.
	Second person	You type.	You type.	You speak.	You speak.
	Third person	He/she/it types.	They type.	He/she/it speaks.	They speak.
PAST	First person	I typed.	We typed.	I spoke.	We spoke.
	Second person	You typed.	You typed.	You spoke.	You spoke.
	Third person	He/she/it typed.	They typed.	He/she/it spoke.	They spoke.
FUTURE	First person	I shall/will type.	We shall/will type.	I shall/will speak.	We shall/will speak.
	Second person	You will type.	You will type.	You will speak.	You will speak.
	Third person	He/she/it will type.	They will type.	He/she/it will speak.	They will speak.
		PERFECT TENSES			
PRESENT	First person	I have typed.	We have typed.	I have spoken.	We have spoken.
	Second person	You have typed.	You have typed.	You have spoken.	You have spoken.
	Third person	He/she/it has typed.	They have typed.	He/she/it has spoken.	They have spoken.
PAST	First person	I had typed.	We had typed.	I had spoken.	We had spoken.
	Second person	You had typed.	You had typed.	You had spoken.	You had spoken.
	Third person	He/she/it had typed.	They had typed.	He/she/it had spoken.	They had spoken.
FUTURE	First person	I shall/will have typed.	We shall/will have typed.	I shall/will have spoken.	We shall/will have spoken.
	Second person	You will have typed.	You will have typed.	You will have spoken.	You will have spoken.
	Third person	He/she/it will have typed.	They will have typed.	He/she/it will have spoken.	They will have spoken.

(Continued)

		REGULAR VERB: TO TYPE		IRREGULAR VERB: TO SPEAK	
		Singular	**Plural**	**Singular**	**Plural**
		PROGRESSIVE TENSES			
PRESENT	First person	I am typing.	We are typing.	I am speaking.	We are speaking.
	Second person	You are typing.	You are typing.	You are speaking.	You are speaking.
	Third person	He/she/it is typing.	They are typing.	He/she/it is speaking.	They are speaking.
PAST	First person	I was typing.	We were typing.	I was speaking.	We were speaking.
	Second person	You were typing.	You were typing.	You were speaking.	You were speaking.
	Third person	He/she/it was typing.	They were typing.	He/she/it was speaking.	They were speaking.
FUTURE	First person	I shall/will be typing.	We shall/will be typing.	I shall/will be speaking.	We shall/will be speaking.
	Second person	You will be typing.	You will be typing.	You will be speaking.	You will be speaking.
	Third person	He/she/it will be typing.	They will be typing.	He/she/it will be speaking.	They will be speaking.
PRESENT PERFECT	First person	I have been typing.	We have been typing.	I have been speaking.	We have been speaking.
	Second person	You have been typing.	You have been typing.	You have been speaking.	You have been speaking.
	Third person	He/she/it has been typing.	They have been typing.	He/she/it has been speaking.	They have been speaking.
PAST PERFECT	First person	I had been typing.	We had been typing.	I had been speaking.	You had been speaking.
	Second person	You had been typing.	You had been typing.	You had been speaking.	You had been speaking.
	Third person	He/she/it had been typing.	They had been typing.	He/she/it had been speaking.	They had been speaking.
FUTURE PERFECT	First person	I shall/will have been typing.	We shall/will have been typing.	I shall/will have been speaking.	We shall/will have been speaking.
	Second person	You will have been typing.	You will have been typing.	You will have been speaking.	You will have been speaking.
	Third person	He/she/it will have been typing.	They will have been typing.	He/she/it will have been speaking.	They will have been speaking.

The practical pay-off in studying tense is learning how to avoid the confusion caused by inappropriate tense shifts, a subject we will consider later (see chapter 9, p. 93). What we need to do now is to get a brief overview of tense,[9] as well as other aspects of verbs known as mood and voice, so that we can move on to the next chapter, where we will see how verbs play their critical role in sentence formation.

For both regular and irregular verbs in the active voice, there are three main groups of tenses: the simple tenses, the perfect tenses and the continuing, or progressive, tenses (or forms). (See p. 42 for a discussion of active and passive voice in verbs.)

Simple tense

The simple tenses refer to action that is completed in the present, the past or the future.

In the present tense, the plain or base form of a verb is used when with the pronouns *I*, *we*, *you* and *they*, and all plural nouns, and the *-s* form of the verb is used with *he*, *she*, *it* and all singular nouns.

> I/we/you/they/the accountants speak.
> He/she/it/the accountant speaks.

The past tense of a verb is formed by combining the plain or basic form with the *-ed* form in regular verbs, and is formed by internal changes in irregular verbs.

> I/you/he/she/it/we/you/they typed.
> I/you/he/she/it/we/you/they spoke.

The future tense of a verb is formed by using *shall* or *will* before the plain form.

> I/you/he/she/it/we/you/they shall/will speak.

Perfect tense

The perfect tenses are used to describe actions which occur at one time but are seen in relation to another time. All are formed by using auxiliaries with the past participle.

The present perfect is formed by using *has* before the past participle for he, she, it and singular nouns, and *have* before the past participle for other pronouns and plural nouns.

> I have typed.
> They have spoken.

The past perfect is formed by using *had* before the past participle.

> You had typed.
> They had spoken.

Progressive tense

The progressive tenses are used to describe actions which are not yet complete within a particular time. They are basically the 'in progress' forms of all three simple tenses (past, present and future) and all three perfect tenses (present perfect, past perfect and future perfect). The progressive tenses are formed by combining the present participle, or *-ing* form of the verb, with the different forms of the auxiliary verb *be* — that is, am/is/are/was/were/will be/have been/has been/had been.

EXERCISE 3.3: TENSES

Read the following sentences and amend verbs where necessary so that they are in the correct tense.
(a) By three o'clock tomorrow, I had typed this document for six hours.
(b) I am speaking to her when Jack walked past.
(c) You will have been typing all day tomorrow.
(d) I had been speaking for more than twenty minutes before I realised the microphone was not working.
(e) I am typing that document just a few minutes ago.

Answers on p. 167.

. . . .

VERBS: FORMS

You should now be familiar with the five basic forms of verbs (table 3.8).

Table 3.8: Verb forms

Plain/base form	type	speak
Past tense	type	spoke
Past participle	typed	spoken
Present participle	typing	speaking
-S form	types	speaks

These five basic forms give us the vital information we need to know about all verbs, regular and irregular. However, there is one major exception to this — the verb *be*, as shown in table 3.9.

Table 3.9: Forms of the verb 'be'

Plain/base form	be
Past tense	was, were
Past participle	been
Present participle	being
-S form	is

To these five forms can be added another two: *am* (I am) and *are* (you/we/you/they are).

The first three forms of all verbs — the plain or base form, the past tense and the past participle — are sometimes known as the *principal parts* of verbs. If you look up a dictionary entry of a verb, you may find that all three principal parts or all five forms are given at the beginning of the entry. Regular verbs will have the *-ed* form for both past tense and past participle (although some dictionary makers will presume that this is understood, and only give the plain base form), while irregular verbs will have the unique forms of past tense and past participle given in full (see figure 3.2).

type /tʌɪp/ v.[1] L16. [f. the n.] **1** v.t. **a** Theol. Foreshadow as a type. L16. **b** Be a symbol of; symbolize. M19. **2** v.t. Be an example of; = TYPIFY 2. rare. E17. **3** v.t. Reproduce by means of type; print. rare. M18. **4** v.t. & i. Write with a typewriter. Also foll. by out, up. L19. **5** v.t. Assign to a particular type; classify; esp. in Biol. & Med., determine the type to which (blood, tissue, etc.) belongs. E20. **6.** v.t. = TYPECAST 2. M20.

4 G. GREENE Mrs Smith typed for him on a portable Corona. A. BURGESS Two cassettes were full and he went .. to type it all out. ANNE STEVENSON Aurelia Plath sat .. typing up her daughter's stories.

 typer n. (arch.) = TYPEWRITER I L19.

speak /spiːk/ v. Pp. t. **spoke** /spəʊk/, (arch. & poet.) **spake** /speɪk/. Pa. pple **spoken** /ˈspəʊk (ə)n/, (arch.) **spoke**. [Late OE specan, superseding parallel OE sprecan which did not survive beyond early ME, = OFris. spreka, OS sprekan, OHG sprehhan (Du. spreken, G sprechen), f. WGmc str. vb w. which cf. ON spraki rumour, forsprakki spokesman.] **I.** v.i. **1 a** Pronounce words, make articulate verbal utterances with the voice; express one's thoughts by words. (Foll. by about, on a subject, to a person, etc.) LOE. **b** Converse; talk with others, with each other, etc. Later also, be on speaking terms. LOE. **c** Deliver a speech or formal address; express one's views in an assembly or to an audience. L16. **d** Propose marriage. arch. E17. **2** Of a writer, literary composition, etc.: make a statement or declaration in words. ME. **3a** Of thunder etc.: make a noise; resound, reverberate. LME. **b** Of a musical instrument etc.: make a sound; spec. emit a full and proper note. E17. **c** Of a firearm: emit a report on being fired. E18. **d** Of a hound: bay or bark; give tongue on finding a scent. E19. **4a** Of a thing: be expressive or significant; make some revelation or disclosure. (Foll. by to.) M16. **b** Take effect legally; be valid. M19.

1a J. WAIN The one who spoke had a broad Lancashire accent. G. BATTISCOMBE William found her very weak and unable to speak distinctly. Encounter No one spoke except about the weather. P. FITZGERALD He must speak to this woman. **b** People We didn't speak for two years. **c** C. V. WEDGWOOD The King, .. allowed to speak before an audience of his people, uttered a .. solemn farewell. E. SEGAL The defence had to speak first and allow the prosecution the last word. **4a** I. MURDOCH There was something .. oriental in their mood, something which spoke .. in the subtly curving mouth.

II v.t. **5a** Articulate, utter (a word, remark, sentence, etc.); make, recite, deliver (a speech or statement); direct or address (words) against, to, etc. LOE. †**b** Use (one's voice) to make an utterance. LME–L16. **6** Utter or express (truth, falsehood, etc.) in words or speech. LOE. **7a** Declare or tell of in words; make known by speech or writing; state that. LOE. **b** Of a musical instrument: announce or proclaim by sound. Chiefly literary. E18. **8a** Talk or converse with; address (a person). arch. LOE. **b** Communicate with (a passing vessel) at sea by signal etc. L18. **9** Use or be able to use as a language; talk (a particular language). ME. **10**†**a** Mention (a person); speak of in a certain way; commend (a person) to another. ME–M17. **b** Bespeak, order. rare. E16. **11** Of a thing: be a sign of, indicate, express; reveal, make known. L16. **b** spec. Of the face, eyes, etc.: indicate or manifest by expression. E17. **12a** Show (a person or thing) to be or do a certain thing or to possess a certain quality. arch. E17. **b** Term, call; describe (as). arch. E17. **13a** Create by speaking. Also foll. by out. rare. M17. **b** Cause to change or enter into another state, condition, or position by speaking. Foll. by into, to, or adj. compl. L17.

5a SHAKES. Meas. for M. Certain words he spoke against your Grace. P. MORTIMER 'You're tired,' he said, the first words he had spoken directly to me for .. weeks. **6** G. GREENE How can I tell that you are speaking the truth? **7a** H. BROOKE You have, in a few words, spoke the whole of the matter. **b** N. ROWE These Trumpets speak his Presence. **9.** R. MACAULAY She .. could speak enough Turkish to get about. D. M. THOMAS Anna could speak three languages besides her native Ukrainian. **10a** SHAKES. Hen. VIII Griffith, give me leave to speak him, And yet with charity. **11** GOLDSMITH The loud laugh that spoke the vacant mind. **b** DRYDEN His face spake hope, while deep his sorrows flow. **12a** SIR W. SCOTT His acquaintance with the English language .. plainly spoke him to be an Englishman. **b** TENNYSON To speak him true, .. No keener hunter after glory breathes. **13b** refl.: New Monthly Magazine He spoke himself into the Common Council.

 Phrases: as they (etc.) **speak** arch. as the phrase is. **know to speak to** have a slight acquaintance with (a person). know whereof one speaks: see WHEREOF 3. †**not to be spoken of** (be) beyond all description. **so to speak** as it were, to a certain extent, in some sense. speak (a person) fair: see FAIR adv. 2. †speak daggers: see DAGGER n.[1] **speak evil or ill of** mention unfavourably, criticize. speak extempore: see EXTEMPORE adv. I. **speak for itself** be significant or self-evident. **speak for oneself** give one's own opinions; speak for yourself, do not presume to speak for others. speak ill of: see speak evil of above. **speak in a person's ear** whisper, speak privately. — **speaking** used by a speaker on the telephone to announce his or her identity. speak in (or with) tongues: see TONGUE n. speak like a book: see BOOK n. speak one's mind: see MIND n.[1] speak out of turn: see TURN n. speak the truth: see TRUTH n. speak volumes: see VOLUME n. **speak well of** mention favourably, praise. **speak-your-weight machine** a weighing machine which announces one's weight in spoken words. **to speak of** worth mentioning (usu. in neg. contexts).

 With advs. & preps. in specialized senses: (See also Phrases above.) **speak for** (a) make a speech or plea in place of or on behalf of (a person); plead for or concerning; (b) (now rare) beg, request; (c) (now usu. in pass.) order; bespeak; engage; (d) indicate, betoken. †**speak forth** utter, declare, proclaim. **speak of** (a) mention or discuss in speech or writing; †(b) rare (Shakes.) bespeak, order; (c) suggest, propose, hint at (doing something). **speak out** (a) utter; make known in words; declare openly or clearly, manifest; (b) talk distinctly or in a loud voice; (c) talk freely or unreservedly; see also sense 13a above. **speak past** talk at cross-purposes with; speak incomprehensibly to. **speak to** (a) approach (a person) for help, service, etc.; bribe; spec. propose marriage to; (b) influence, affect, touch; (c) deal with, discuss, or comment on (a subject) in speech or writing; (d) give evidence regarding (a thing), attest; (e) address with censure or reproof, admonish; (f) (of a hound) give indications of (a fox, scent, etc.) by baying or barking. **speak together** hold consultation; confer. **speak up** (a) raise one's voice; (begin to) talk boldly or unreservedly; (b) speak up for, speak firmly on behalf of or in defence of. **speak with** Naut. communicate with (another vessel); see also sense 1b above.

 Comb.: **speak-back** = talkback s.v. TALK v.; **speak-box** an intercom device which allows a caller to speak to someone elsewhere in a building; **speakeasy** slang (chiefly US, now Hist.) a shop or drinking club selling alcoholic liquor illegally during Prohibition; **speak-house** (a) Hist. a room in a convent or monastery where conversation was permitted or visitors received; (b) in the S. Pacific islands, a large hut used as a place of council.

Figure 3.2: Dictionary entries for type and speak.

(Source: The New Shorter Oxford Dictionary (1993: 3441, 2969–2970) Oxford: Oxford University Press. Reproduced with permission.)

VERBS: MOOD

The intentions of a writer or speaker can be shown in the mood of a verb. There are three moods:

1. Indicative — used to make a statement or ask a question. This is the most common mood.

> I typed the letter.
> Are you speaking?

2. Imperative — used to give commands and make requests.

> Type that letter now.
> Please speak at the meeting.
> Speak!

3. Subjunctive — used to express a desire, wish or plan that may be unlikely or at least conditional.

> If I were you, I would type it up before she arrives.
> The board has asked that he speak to the members.

The auxiliary verbs are particularly useful for expressing mood. For example: can (indicative), must (imperative), may (subjunctive).

There is considerable disagreement about whether we should even bother with the subjunctive mood in particular, and with the whole concept of mood in general. While mood is important in other languages, it is not a major concept in English.[10] Nevertheless, awareness of mood can provide some useful subtleties in expression (note the section on shifts in mood, p. 95).

VERBS: ACTIVE AND PASSIVE VOICE

Consider these two sentences:

> Mary typed the letter.
> The letter was typed by Mary.

The first sentence features a verb in the *active voice*, while the second features a verb in the *passive voice*. A verb in the active voice is one whose subject performs the action in a sentence. A verb in the passive voice is one whose subject is acted upon, or receives the action named by the verb.

Only transitive verbs (those taking a direct object) can be changed from active to passive voice. In passive-voice sentences, the person or thing performing the action often appears as the object of the preposition *by*, but is sometimes omitted altogether. Passive-voice sentences use a form of *be*, together with the past participle of the main verb.

Passive voice	Active voice
The fax was sent by Lim.	Lim sent the fax.
Your performance is being monitored.	(They are) monitoring your performance.
The words will be spoken by Jane.	Jane will speak the words.

There are a few particular circumstances where the passive voice is preferable to the active voice. It is useful, for example, where the actor or subject of a sentence is unknown, or is relatively unimportant:

The dinosaurs were eliminated from the face of the earth.
These cartons are delivered daily.

In most circumstances, however, it is preferable to use the active voice rather than the passive. Active voice sentences are shorter, more direct and more personal. For these very reasons, it has almost become a cliché that sentences emerging from faceless bureaucracies are usually in the passive voice — precisely because the writers of such sentences can thus remain anonymous and avoid any responsibility for the actions described in the sentence.

Evasive passive	Direct active
The report was submitted late.	I submitted the report late.
Your goods appear to have been lost.	We have lost your goods.
Mistakes have been made.	We made mistakes.
Attempts should be made to complete this form correctly if delays are to be avoided.	You should attempt to complete this form correctly if you wish to avoid delays.
It was decided that she would be dismissed.	We decided to dismiss her.

Notice that the evasive possessive is not formed by simply reversing the order of the direct active. The actors (I/We/We/You/We) are conveniently dropped altogether. The evasive passive is thus not the personal passive, but the impersonal passive.

In many organisations, the people who set the house-style rules and/ or shape the organisational culture still prefer the passive voice, as the active voice and the personal pronouns which accompany them are seen, not so much as signs of clear and direct communication, as signs of attention-seeking or egotistical communication. Fortunately, this is becoming less true: enlightened decision-makers today need to empower employees with more direct responsibility if the customers of organisations are to be better served, and such decision-makers realise that an apparently superficial thing such as the voice used in official communications can be an important part of such a strategy. Flowing from this, they realise that it might be better to risk a bit of spotlight-grabbing in communication if it means that the bureaucratic evasiveness and dishonesty of 'the pussyfooting passive'[11] will be flushed out of the system.

Occasionally, of course, directness may not be the most direct way of achieving things. A tactful 'This report appears to need more work' may get you the result you require, whereas a confrontational 'You need to re-do this report' may be more likely to evoke a hostile response. The passive can thus be a tool of tactfulness, but care must be taken — you should take care — to ensure that the occasional use of tact does not become the consistent use of hypocrisy and cowardice.

The passive voice also has been used traditionally in scientific and technological writing, although even in that communication arena things are changing rapidly.[12]

Note also the relationship between the passive voice and disjuncts or sentence modifiers (p. 189).

EXERCISE 3.4:

VOICE

Change the following passive-voice sentences into active voice, and active-voice sentences into passive voice.
(a) A million dollars has been won by us in the lottery!
(b) You must re-type this letter.
(c) The document was given to us by Sven.
(d) Policy documents like these are expected to be read more easily.
(e) Care should be taken to ensure that appropriate warnings are given.

Answers on p. 167.

• •

PROBLEM VERBS: LAY/LIE, RAISE/RISE, SET/SIT, HANG/HANG

Confusion often arises when people need to choose between *lay* or *lie*, *set* or *sit*, *raise* or *rise*, and *hang* (suspend) or *hang* (execute). This confusion arises because in the first three pairs, one verb is transitive and the other is intransitive, while confusion arises with *hang/hang* because we are in fact dealing with two verbs, not one, with one being regular and one being irregular in structure. Let's look at the different forms of these eight verbs in table 3.10.

Table 3.10: Different forms of verbs

Simple/base form	Past tense	Past participle
lay	laid	laid
lie	lay	lain
raise	raised	raised
rise	rose	risen
sit	sat	sat
set	set	set
hang (execute, commit suicide)	hanged	hanged
hang (suspend)	hung	hung

Notice that *sit*, *set*, *lie*, *lay* and *rose* are all irregular verbs, while *rise* is a regular verb (a regular verb being one which forms its past tense and past participle by adding *-d* or *-ed* to its plain, base, simple or dictionary form). The regular or irregular nature of these verbs is not the cause of confusion, however.

Lay, *raise* and *set* are transitive (T) verbs — that is, they take a direct object, while *lie*,* *rise* and *sit* are intransitive (IT) verbs — that is, they do not take a direct object. We can determine which is which by deciding on what meaning we need to convey (see table 3.11).

Table 3.11: Examples of transitive and intransitive verbs

Typical sentence	Verb	Direct object?	Verb type
You'd better lie down.	lie	no	IT
I'll lay that carpet tomorrow.	lay	yes	T
On weekends, I rise at a later time.	rise	no	IT
They raised the flag.	raise	yes	T
Please sit down.	sit	no	IT
Please set the table.	set	yes	T

Words or phrases which accompany intransitive verbs are not direct objects but adverbs or prepositional phrases — that is, modifiers. (Note that *set* does in fact behave intransitively when used to describe suns/ stars, planets and moons setting).

Do we *hang* a picture or *hang* a person? We do both. Problems arise not so much in the present-tense forms as in the past tense and past participle.

We *hung* the picture opposite the window.
The executioner *hanged* him.

EXERCISE 3.5:

PROBLEM VERBS

Consider the verbs in italics in the following sentences. If they are incorrect, mark them with a cross, and correct them. If they are correct, tick them, and leave them as is.

(a) She *set* on the settee where I *lay* injured, and *sat* my leg in splints.
(b) The gardener had *risen* the pot of rose cuttings to a higher shelf.
(c) I don't know whether these eggs are freshly *lain* or not, so I'll just have to *lie* if they ask me about them.
(d) The paintings of the tarot card figures had been vandalised, particularly the one of the *Hung* Man which had been *hung* near the alcove.
(e) Laden with worries, I *laid* on the settee, watching as the sun *rise* and *set*.

Answers on p. 167.

● ●

---

* **Lie** — to recline — should not be confused with the regular verb, **lie** — to tell an untruth.

LANGUAGE: THE LIGHTER SIDE

Learn to write goodly

1. Don't use no double negatives.
2. Make each pronoun agree with their antecedent.
3. Join clauses good, like a conjunction should.
4. About them sentence fragments.
5. When dangling, watch your participles.
6. Verbs has to agree with their subject.
7. Just between you and I, case is important to.
8. Don't write run-on sentences they are hard to read.
9. Don't use commas, which aren't necessary.
10. Try not to oversplit infinitives.
11. It is important to use your apostrophe's correctly.
12. Proofread your writing to if any words out.
13. Correct spelling is esential.

Apostrophe's and other matters

It's is not, it isn't ain't, and it's it's, not its, if you mean it is. If you don't, it's its. Then too, it's hers. It isn't her's. It isn't our's, either. It's ours, and likewise yours and theirs.

Some (rather irregular) irregular verbs

The game of 'Irregular Verbs' or 'Conjugations' was begun by the British philosopher, Bertrand Russell. In conventional grammar analysis, when studying English or another language, it is useful to use the basic technique of declining or conjugating a verb, a process which at its most basic level shows the form of the verb in the first, second and third person singular: I sing, you sing, he sings/is singing. 'Irregular verbs' is a parody of this process wherein the person doing the declining of the 'irregular verbs' makes (humorously) bogus distinctions between the first, second and third persons.

- I am firm; you are obstinate; he is a pig-headed fool.
- I am an epicure; you are a gourmand; he has both feet in the trough.
- I am sparkling; you are unusually talkative; he is drunk.
- I am far-seeing; you are a visionary; he's a fuzzy-minded dreamer.
- I am beautiful; you have quite good features; she isn't bad-looking, if you like that type.
- I have reconsidered; you have changed your mind; he has gone back on his word.
- I dream; you escape; he needs help.
- I am at my prime; you are middle-aged; he's getting old.
- I am a liberal; you are a radical; he is a communist.
- I am casual; you are informal; he is an unshaven slob.

- I am in charge of public relations; you exaggerate; he misleads.
- I am a camera; you are a copycat; he is a plagiarist.
- I am righteously indignant; you are annoyed; he is making a fuss about nothing.
- I am a behavioural researcher; you are curious about people; he is a Peeping Tom.
- I am nostalgic; you are old-fashioned; he is living in the past.

Listen! I'm one run-on sentence from the time I was born 'till the day I die! Very little punctuation! I just keep nattering away . . . until I strike a thought. You know what I'm saying? Sooner or later I will strike a good thought, but you just gotta keep talking 'till that happens.

Mel Brooks

On the use of the royal/editorial plural

Only kings, editors and people with tapeworm have the right to use the editorial 'we.'

Mark Twain

BUILDING SENTENCES

What is a sentence? In this chapter we will combine the information we have acquired thus far with new information to provide a satisfactory answer to this question. Understanding the ways in which sentences work — and, perhaps, more to the point, don't work — is a critical part of becoming a better communicator.

We will start with what we know already about subject and predicate and verbs, and go on to consider phrases, clauses and sentence types.

INDIRECT OBJECTS, OBJECT COMPLEMENTS AND APPOSITIVES

We have learned earlier (p. 26) about transitive verbs and direct objects, and linking (being) verbs and subject complements, and their role in forming sentences. We need now to acquaint ourselves with some other parts of the sentence, namely indirect objects, object complements and appositives.

Indirect objects

We have learned so far that basic sentences are structured thus:

I read books.   I = subject
read = verb
books = direct object
read books = predicate

Read here, of course, is behaving as a transitive verb — a transitive verb being a verb that has a direct impact upon a person or thing in the predicate (whereas an intransitive verb does not have a direct impact upon a person or thing in the predicate).

Now consider this sentence:

The manager gave Bert a gold watch.

'Manager' is the subject, 'gave' is the verb, 'a gold watch' is the direct object, the predicate is 'gave Bert a gold watch', but what function does 'Bert' perform? The proper noun 'Bert' here is an *indirect object*.

The *direct object* completes the meaning of a transitive verb — it tells us *what* about the verb.

Gave what? — a gold watch.

The *indirect object* names the person or thing affected by the action of the verb — it answers the question *to whom?*[*] or the question *for whom?* about the verb.

Gave the gold watch to whom? — to Bert.

Let's look at some other examples of this type of sentence in table 4.1.

Table 4.1: Examples of sentences with indirect objects

SUBJECT	PREDICATE		
	Verb	**Indirect object** (answers question 'to/for whom?')	**Direct object** (answers question 'what?')
She	gave	the old man	directions.
I	told	her	the truth.
The heroic general	gave	his troops	his opinion.

Complements

When we were considering transitive verbs earlier (p. 26), we looked at direct objects. Now we should be familiar with both direct objects and indirect objects in sentences.

We know that there are verbs of action and being, and transitive and intransitive verbs are action verbs. When we were looking at *being* verbs earlier (p. 28), we saw that such verbs — be, remain, seem, sound, and so on — cannot form predicates on their own, because they cannot be transitive — they cannot have a direct object. Such verbs act as linking verbs with *subject complements*, linking the sentence subjects to the description that follows:

Table 4.2: Examples of sentences with subject complements

SUBJECT	PREDICATE		
	Linking verb	**Subject complement**	**Subject complement type**
She	was	supervisor.	predicate noun
She	was	angry.	predicate adjective

---

[*] Who or whom? What's the difference? We will find this out on p. 70.

The direct object of an action verb can also take a complement, known as an *object complement*. Such an object complement can complete the meaning of the direct object.

Table 4.3: Examples of sentences with object complements

SUBJECT	PREDICATE		
	Transitive verb	**Direct object**	**Object complement**
She	considered	the exam	useless.
The people	elected	him	President.
Christmas time	makes	children	happy.

Appositives

An appositive is a word or group of words that renames a noun:

The manager, *Natalie Wakefield*, was new in the job.
The only staff member she knew, *an accountant*, was not always available for advice.

EXERCISE 4.1:

SENTENCE PARTS

Consider the sentences below. Identify the italicised parts as direct object (DO), indirect object (IO), subject complement (SC), object complement (OC) or appositive (A).

(a) She was *unhappy.*
(b) I considered her *a friend*.
(c) She offered him *a promotion*.
(d) She offered *him* a promotion.
(e) Her brother, *a non-member*, was excluded.

Answers on p. 167.

• •

PHRASES

A phrase is a group of two or more related words that lacks either a subject or predicate or both. A phrase may contain a verb, but the verb will be a non-finite one (infinitive, gerund, present participle, past participle).

We have already come across prepositional phrases (p. 22), but we now need to look at the full range of phrase types. The major types of phrases are prepositional, participial, gerund, infinitive and absolute (see table 4.4). Understanding the way these phrases work can help us to construct better sentences, and in particular can help us avoid making mistakes which can lead to ambiguity or confusion about the meaning of sentences.

Table 4.4: Types of phrases

Phrase type	Example	Composition	Analysis
1. Prepositional	I walked *over that bridge.*	preposition plus object plus any modifiers	functions as adverb, modifying verbs, adjectives or adverbs (here, *walked*)
	I like the bridge *near the freeway.*	preposition plus object plus any modifiers	functions as adjective, modifying nouns or pronouns (here, *bridge*)
2. Participial	*Walking down the street,* he noticed her there.	present participle (-*ing* form of verb) plus its modifiers and/or its object (note that prepositional phrase *down the street* acts as a modifier)	functions as an adjective, modifying nouns or pronouns (here, *he*: sentence subject)
	Opened only yesterday, the store has already attracted many customers.	past participle (-*ed* form of regular verbs; various forms of irregular verbs) plus modifiers and/or its object)	functions as an adjective, modifying nouns or pronouns (here, *store*: sentence subject)
3. Gerund	*Walking down the street* is his favourite exercise.	gerund (-*ing* form of verb) plus its modifiers and/or its object	functions as a noun (here, subject of verb *is*)
	His favourite exercise is *walking down the street.*		functions as a noun (here, object of verb *is*)
4. Infinitive	*To win the prize* is my dream.	infinitive plus modifiers and/or its object	functions as noun (here, subject of verb *is*)
	I hope *to win the prize.*		functions as noun (here, object of verb *hope*)
	This is the best software package *to improve productivity.*		functions as adjective (here, modifying noun *package*)
	We were concerned *to improve productivity.*		functions as adverb (here, modifying adjective *concerned*)
5. Absolute	*Training funds now being available,* she was able to improve her knowledge of spreadsheets.	noun or pronoun plus participle plus modifiers	modifies entire sentence; contains a subject (here, *funds*). Participles which are forms of *be* (*being, having been*) are sometimes omitted.

EXERCISE 4.2:

PHRASES

Consider the phrases underlined in the passage below. Complete table 4.5 and identify phrase types, composition patterns and structural functions.

Strolling nonchalantly in, she failed to notice the time on the clock on the wall. The expression on her face being aggressive, she sat down at her console. Arriving late was her only shortcoming, but her career will be out the window unless she arrives on time more often. To get here on time is normal behaviour, not something that is beyond the call of duty.

Answers on p. 168.

Table 4.5: Phrase analysis

Phrase	Type	Composition	Analysis
1. Strolling nonchalantly in			
2. to notice the time			
3. on the clock			
4. on the wall			
5. The expression on her face being aggressive			
6. at her console			
7. Arriving late			
8. out the window			
9. on time			
10. To get here on time			
11. beyond the call of duty			

EXERCISE 4.3:

PHRASES AGAIN

Write ten sentences, each containing at least two different types of phrases. (Ensure that you cover all types of phrases within the range of the ten sentences.) Draw up a table similar to table 4.5, and analyse all phrases in detail.

CLAUSES

We know now that a phrase is a group of two or more related words that lacks either a subject or predicate or both. A phrase may contain a verb, but the verb will be a non-finite one (infinitive, gerund, present participle, past participle).

A clause is the next most complex building block used when constructing sentences. A clause is a group of two or more related words that contains both a subject and a predicate. A clause contains a finite verb — 'finite' in the sense that it is limited, or finite, in relation to subject, person, number and tense (or time). This means, in effect, that a finite verb changes according to its subject, person, number and tense.

There are two types of clauses — independent clauses and dependent clauses. An independent or main clause is a self-contained unit of meaning:

> I like tofu.
> You prefer steak.

An independent clause, in fact, can stand as a sentence by itself. Independent clauses can also be linked by basic conjunctions — and, but, and others — to form sentences:

> I like tofu, but you like steak.

The structure of this sentence, shown in table 4.6, is fairly clear:

Table 4.6: Example of a sentence with independent clauses

Subject	Predicate		Conjunction	Subject	Predicate	
	Finite verb	Object			Finite verb	Object
I	like	tofu	but	you	like	steak

The independent clauses are sentences within the sentence, or are *embedded sentences.*[13]

A dependent clause or subordinate clause, on the other hand, is not self-contained — is not 'finished':

> Although you can't stand the stuff

To work properly within a sentence, a dependent clause needs an independent clause:

> I like tofu, although you can't stand the stuff.

Dependent clauses are of four types: adverb clauses, adjective clauses, noun clauses and elliptical clauses. We can often tell whether a clause is a particular type of dependent clause, or indeed whether it is an independent clause, by the words used to link it to other parts of a sentence (table 4.7).

Table 4.7: Connecting words

Connector type	Examples	Function	Examples in sentences
1. Coordinating conjunctions	For/and/nor/ but/or/yet/so	join two or more grammatically equivalent units	
	and/but/nor/or/ yet	join any two or more grammatically equivalent units: noun + noun, verb + verb, adjective + adjective, adverb + adverb, phrase + phrase, dependent clause + dependent clause, independent clause + independent clause	• Jack *and* Jill • twist *and* shout • to be *or* not to be • cruel *but* fair • quickly *or* slowly • on your feet *or* on your knees • working with them *yet* despising them • He cannot find anyone now, *nor* does he expect to find anyone in the future*.
	for/so (*for* may also work as a preposition)	can only connect independent clauses	• you'll need some help, *for* those tasks are complex. • it was available, *so* I used it.
2. Correlative junctions	both . . . and neither . . . nor either . . . or not only . . . but also as . . . as whether . . . or not . . . but	join two grammatically equivalent units; work in pairs	• both black *and* white • *neither* up *nor* down • He was *not only* working there *but also* sleeping there.
3. Subordinate conjunctions	after /although/as/ as long as/ because/before/ even if/even though/if/if only/in order that/now that/ once/provided that/ rather than /since/ so that/though/ unless/until/when / where/whether/ while	begin certain (adverbial) dependent clauses	• *although* you can't stand the stuff • *wherever* he went • *rather* than her doing likewise

* 'Nor is likewise required when a negation is carried over into the second of two independent clauses, in which case it also triggers inversion of the subject and the auxiliary verb in the second clause.' *American Heritage Dictionary* (1992:1233)

Connector type	Examples	Function	Examples in sentences
4. Relative pronouns	who/whose/ whom/whoever/ whomever/which/ that/what/ whatever	begin certain (adjectival and noun) dependent clauses. Refers to a noun or pronoun in the independent clause	• *who* are illiterate • *which* is insulated against power surges
5. Conjunctive adverbs	accordingly/also/ anyhow/anyway/ besides/ consequently/ furthermore/ hence/however/ indeed/ meanwhile/ moreover/namely/ nevertheless/ similarly/still/ therefore/thus	link independent clauses only. Usually follow a semicolon	• She has the qualifications; *consequently,* she must be considered to be a candidate for the job.

Let's now examine the differing forms of the four main types of dependent clauses. Following the pattern established with the analysis of phrases, table 4.8 shows us examples of such dependent clauses, their composition, and some analysis of their functions.

Table 4.8: Types of dependent clauses

Dependent clause type	Example	Composition	Analysis
1. Adverb clause			• modifies verbs, adverbs, adjectives, independent clauses. • tells us when, where, why, how, under what conditions, with what result, etc.[14]
	He protested *when I cut the budget*.	begins with subordinate conjunction	modifies verb *protested*
	Move it across *until I say 'stop'*.	begins with subordinate conjunction	modifies adverb *across*[15]
	The space was empty *where her desk had been*.	begins with subordinate conjunction	modifies adjective *empty*
	Because he didn't have the right connections, James didn't get the job.	begins with subordinate conjunction	modifies entire independent clause *James didn't get the job*

(Continued)

Dependent clause type	Example	Composition	Analysis
2. Adjective clause			• modifies nouns, pronouns • tells us who or what
	The shop *which sells stationery* was closed.	begins with relative pronoun, which relates to antecedent in independent clause	modifies noun *shop*
	I'll catch him, *whoever he is.*	begins with relative pronoun, which relates to antecedent in independent clause	modifies pronoun *him*
3. Noun clause			functions as a noun; can be subject, predicate noun, object of a verb, or object of a preposition
	What the world needs now is love.	begins with relative pronoun, or with *when, where, whether, why* and *how*	functions as a noun; subject of verb *is*[16]
	We agreed *that we would stay.*	begins with relative pronoun, or with *when, where, whether, why* and *how*	functions as a noun; object of verb *agreed*
	That is *when we said no.*	begins with relative pronoun, or with *when, where, whether, why* and *how*	functions as a noun; predicate noun/complement
	We drove to *where the plane was expected to land.*	begins with relative pronoun, or with *when, where, whether, why* and *how*	functions as a noun; object of preposition *to*
4. Elliptical clauses			clauses in which omissions or ellipses have occurred
	This is the song *I like best.*	• occurs in adjectival clauses • relative pronoun *which/that* omitted; presumed to be understood • relates to antecedent in independent clause	modifies noun *song*
	Though (they were) sceptical, management decided to fund the project.	• occurs in adverbial clauses • subject and verb omitted	modifies noun *management*
	The desktop computer was performing better *than the mainframe* (was performing)	second half of the comparison omitted	modifies *computer*

Underline dependent clauses in the following sentences. Identify them as adverbial, adjectival, noun or elliptical.

(a) He will be happy once it is in the mail.

(b) Whether we stay or go is the real question.

(c) This is the document which is the source of all the controversy.

(d) I think that you are wrong.

(e) Unless you apply by the due date, I can't guarantee anything.

(f) Even if dubious, you should still consider that proposal.

(g) Mary told me that you wouldn't be coming.

(h) Although I had arrived early, they went without me.

(i) Give me something that I can believe in.

(j) An upgraded computer is what we want.

Answers on p. 169.

Write twenty sentences, comprising:

(a) five sentences containing adverbial clauses

(b) five sentences containing adjectival clauses

(c) five sentences containing noun clauses

(d) five sentences containing elliptical clauses.

- -

SENTENCE TYPES

Now we should have a good overview of phrases and clauses. Let's go on to look at the different types of sentences, namely, simple sentences, compound sentences, complex sentences and compound-complex sentences. Table 4.9 repeats the pattern of analysis established when we considered phrases and clauses.

Table 4.9: Types of sentences

Sentence type	Example	Composition	Analysis
1. Simple		• contains one independent clause • contains no dependent clause • may contain phrases • may have compound subjects, verbs and objects	
	Birds fly.		• subject *birds* • finite verb *fly*
	For the record, both eagles and hawks cover enormous distances along the traditional summer migratory routes.		• compound subject *eagles and hawks* • finite verb *cover* • phrases *for …, along …*
	The hawk soars to great heights and then swoops down on its prey.		• subject *hawk* • compound predicates *soars to great heights, swoops down on its prey*

(Continued)

Sentence type	Example	Composition	Analysis
2. Compound		• two or more independent clauses • contains no dependent clauses • clauses may be joined by: —coordinating conjunction (*for, and, nor, but, or, yet, so*) + —comma —semicolon —conjunctive adverb (*accordingly, consequently, however,* etc.) and semicolon —colon	
	The hawk is a small bird, but the eagle is a large bird.		independent clause + conjunction + independent clause
	The hawk is a small bird; the eagle is a large bird.		independent clause + (;) + independent clause
	The hawk can move extremely quickly; consequently, it is able to catch faster-moving prey.		independent clause + (;) + conjunctive adverb + independent clause
3. Complex		• contains one independent clause • contains one or more subordinate clauses • dependent clauses before independent clauses take a comma	
	While the eagle is a diurnal creature, the eagle owl is nocturnal.		dependent clause + independent clause
	The eagle owl hunts by night, although its namesake hunts by day.		independent clause + dependent clause
	Birds which hunt at night have an advantage, as prey is less likely to detect them.		independent clause containing dependent clause (*which hunt at night*) + dependent clause

Sentence type	Example	Composition	Analysis
4. Compound-complex		• contains two or more independent clauses • contains at least one subordinate clause	
	While many species of animals have not developed defences against nocturnal predators, some species have developed good night vision and others have developed camouflage markings.		dependent clause + independent clause + independent clause
	Hawks can fly great distances, and eagles can fly similar distances, provided that they can take prey regularly.		independent clause + independent clause + dependent clause

EXERCISE 4.6:

SENTENCES

Identify each of the following sentences as simple, compound, complex or compound-complex.

(a) I fell down the stairs, but she remained on her feet.

(b) Although the figures were in on time, Malcolm was still critical of the project, and head office disputed their validity anyway.

(c) I was only talking to her.

(d) Walking down the street, I was surprised to see a giant balloon overhead.

(e) The figures which she wanted are here, although I can't see any mention of Malaysian exports in them.

Answers on p. 169.

• •

EXERCISE 4.7:

SENTENCES AGAIN

Write a story, memo or letter of twelve sentences in length. The sequence of the sentences should be arranged thus:

Sentence number	Sentence type
1, 5, 9	Simple
2, 6, 10	Compound
3, 7, 11	Complex
4, 8, 12	Compound-complex

• •

THOSE (EXPLETIVE DELETED) EXPLETIVES!

The word 'expletive' describes words that are added to a sentence to fill it out, without adding much to the meaning. This can mean exclamations or oaths — sometimes obscene or profane ones[*] — and it can also mean word groups such as *it is*, *there are* and *there is*. *It* looks like a pronoun, but it's not: it doesn't refer to any antecedent noun or pronoun. *There* looks like an adverb, but it isn't: it doesn't answer the question 'where?' In fact, an expletive has no grammatical function at all — it is certainly not the subject of a sentence. The expletive is just there to get the sentence started, which probably means that the sentence is too wordy, and the meaning is less direct than it should be.[17]

Compare, for example, the following sentence.

> *There are* many people in the cafeteria today.

A more direct (and shorter) way of putting this might be:

> Many people are in the cafeteria today.

Consider also another sentence, and then the same sentence re-cast, without the expletive beginning:

> *It is* not clear whether or not we will get a seat.
> Whether we will get a seat or not is not clear.

Expletives can sometimes help get sentences started, but try to avoid them. They have much in common with passive voice constructions (p. 42), and disjuncts (p. 89) — all make your writing more vague and less personal.

'There will be no *@!!*? whitewash in the *!!@?? White House...

---

[*] The term 'expletive deleted' (meaning obscenities deleted so as not to offend the reader) was used when transcripts of the taped conversations of US President Richard Nixon and his staff were published in 1974 as part of the enquiry into the Watergate hotel break-in in 1972.

SENTENCE FRAGMENTS

We now should have a fairly clear idea of what a sentence is. A sentence is a group of words which:

- has a subject
- has a finite verb
- does not begin with a subordinating conjunction or a relative pronoun
- is punctuated with an initial capital letter and some form of end punctuation (see p. 102).

If a group of words does not meet these critieria, but is punctuated as if it were a complete sentence, then it is in fact a *sentence fragment*. Let's consider some of these fragments and some possible ways to overcome their shortcomings. Fragments, faults and possible revisions are contained in table 4.10.

Table 4.10: Sentence fragments and revisions

Sentence fragment	Fault	Possible revision
Walked down the street.	no subject	We walked down the street.
Walking down the street.	participial phrase only — finite verb needed	Walking down the street, he thought about the problem./ We were walking down the street/We walked down the street.
To walk down the street.	infinitive phrase only — finite verb needed	We decided to walk down the street.
We were able to catch the courier at the lights. *By walking down the street.*	prepositional phrase only — finite verb and subject needed	By walking down the street, we were able to catch the courier at the lights.
He saw the whole thing. *Because he was walking down the street.*	dependent clause only — beginning with subordinate conjunction. Independent clause needed	Because he was walking down the street, he saw the whole thing.
He saw the whole thing. *The employee who was walking down the street.*	most of fragment is a dependent clause only — beginning with a relative pronoun. Independent clause needed	The employee who was walking down the street saw the whole thing.

EXERCISE 4.8:

EXPLETIVES AND FRAGMENTS

Reconstruct the following sentences, removing expletives and fragments.

(a) There are many reasons I can think of as to why she shouldn't go.

(b) It is not clear at this stage just what my role is.

(c) It was in September that I first met her.

(d) There were many people walking to the festival that day.

(e) It was regrettable that she was unable to pay.

(f) Breathing in the ocean air.

(g) To play in the sand.

(h) He watched her. Combing her hair.

(i) She didn't like the music. Because it was too loud.

(j) The artist sketching. Using charcoal.

Suggested answers on p. 169.

TALKING POINTS

BREAKING THE RULES: Verbless sentences

Do all sentences need to contain a verb? H. W. Fowler below considers the exceptions to this apparent rule.

> Remember, such verbless sentences are created by experienced writers. To break the rules in this fashion, you need to know what the rules are, so don't confuse style with sloppiness. If you are still getting your writing skills under control, avoid the fragmented effect of verbless sentences, because your audience may believe that such fragments are proof that you are a sloppy, rather than a stylish writer.

A grammarian might say that a verbless sentence was a contradiction in terms; but ... the definition of a sentence is that which the OED (*Oxford English Dictionary*) calls 'in popular use often, such a portion of a composition or utterance as extends from one full stop to another.'

The verbless sentence is a device for enlivening the written word by approximating it to the spoken. There is nothing new about it. Tacitus,[*] for one was much given to it. What is new is its vogue with English journalists and other writers, and it may be worthwhile to attempt some analysis of the purpose it is intended to serve (see table 4.11).

Table 4.11: Verbless sentences

Sentence type	Rationale	Example
1. Transitional	may contain a summary comment on what has gone before	• *True, no doubt.* • *So far, so good.* • *Of course not.*
	may introduce what is to follow	• *The practical conclusion?* • *Finally on one small point.* • *Lastly the poetry of metaphor.*
2. Afterthought	use of a full stop instead of lighter punctuation may suggest a pause for reflection	• *Among living novelists, E. M. Forster, I. Compton Burnett and Angus Wilson have done this. And C. P. Snow.* • *Some lines might have been written by Auden himself. Well almost.* • *He thought as much as he observed. More in fact.* • *Mr Laughton shuffles about the stage, apple-cheeked and rosy, looking very like Mr Boffin in fancy dress. Yet not altogether like Mr Boffin, neither.*
3. Dramatic climax		• *The winter seas, endlessly hammering, endlessly probing for a weakness, had found one. The cement.* • *The intruder was no gay young man, but a grey-haired naval captain with one eye and one arm. Nelson.* • *Unless something is done soon, Oxford, the home of lost causes, will lose the last cause of all. Oxford itself.* • *We shall face difficulties as we have always done. As a united nation.*
4. Comment	especially if arch or strident or intended to surprise	• *We solved the whole thing by appointing a Royal Commission. A neat solution. Clever us.* • *I could make my own survey on this new social phenomenon. A sort of Kinsey Report.* • *From Mr K. down to the simplest party unit, the goal is simply 'Produce or die'. Recipe à la Danton.*

(Continued)

[*] Publius Cornelius Tacitus (AD 55?–120?). Roman public official and author of two famous Latin works, the *Histories* and the *Annals*.

Sentence type	Rationale	Example
5. Pictorial	(This quotation is aptly described by a reviewer of the book from which it is taken as an example of the 'verbless convulsive'.)	• The courteous inquisitor of television eyed me across his plain brown deal table. Politely. Courteously. Unaggressively. • Here silence and beauty were absolute. No aeroplane. Not even tree. • Eel Pie Island is like the Deep South. The same feeling of soft dereliction. The Thames green and dulled — a New Orleans bayou? The moon a silver magnolia. • And now the copse is thinned out. No badgers. No tramps. • It is an entire streetful of shops. Complete with side arcades. And two snack bars. All piled on top of another. A whole civilization all to itself. Practically a state.
6. Aggressive		The particular dynamism of the publishing group which this book concerns springs, of course, from the rumbustious school of journalism it nurtured. Defying the conventions. Hastening the inevitable in social change. Cocking a snook at the hoary traditions and pomposities of our times. Fighting the taboos.

Lastly here are a few examples, from the many that might be given, of verbless sentences that do not lend themselves to classification but are, it seems, merely the product of a writer's conviction that the more staccato the style the livelier the effect.

— Now we are getting on to weaker ground. And a script. Alas, the script.

— He receives no official praise or reproof. A freelance.

— So it will be a miracle if we get our restoration. Undoubtedly.

— She makes sure the conversation is gay, witty and light. But business.

— Some see the League trying to become independent. Unlikely.

— He hasn't got the proper mind for legal technicalities. Too much commonsense.

Since the verbless sentence is freely employed by some good writers (as well as extravagantly by many less good ones) it must be classed as modern English usage. That grammarians may deny it the right to be called a sentence has nothing to do with its merits. It must be judged by its success in affecting the reader in the way the writer intended. Used sparingly and with discrimination, the device can no doubt be an effective medium of emphasis, intimacy, and rhetoric. Overdone, as it is in the sprightlier sort of modern journalism, it gets on a reader's nerves, offending against the principle of good writing immortalised in Flaubert's aphorism '*L'auteur, dans son œuvre, doit être comme Dieu dans l'univers, présent partout et visible nulle part.*' ('The writer, in his work, must be like God in the universe — present everywhere and visible nowhere.')

Adapted with permission from Fowler, H. W. , *A Dictionary of Modern English Usage* (Second Edition. Revised by Sir Ernest Gowers) (London: Book Club Associates/Oxford University Press, 1990: 674–676).

CASE

Consider the following sentences:

Who/whom does this belong to?
He gave the papers to John and I/me?

Which of the alternatives — who/whom, I/me — is correct?

To answer this question, we need to know more about the *case* of nouns and pronouns. The case of a word lets us know what role the word is playing in a sentence. Is it an object, or subject? Is it being used to show ownership or possession of something?

There are three cases which are used in English, although other languages use more. The three cases are subjective, objective and possessive. (This is American usage. British usage is to use the more traditional, Latin-based terms of nominative [subjective], accusative [objective] and genitive [possessive.)[18] Let's have a look at the way these three cases work in table 5.1.

If a pronoun works as the subject of a sentence, then it takes subjective case:

She wrote to me.
I wrote to her.

Pronouns in the objective case can operate as direct objects or indirect objects:

Maria gave the report to *him*.
Maria gave *him* the report.

If possession or ownership needs to be shown, then pronouns in the possessive case are used.

Her car was brand new.
The car was hers.
The rewards for finishing the project on time were all ours.
The rewards are theirs, and theirs alone.

Table 5.1: Case in nouns and pronouns[19]

		SUBJECTIVE	OBJECTIVE	POSSESSIVE
Nouns				
SINGULAR		boy	boy	boy's
		child	child	child's
PLURAL		boys	boys	boys'
		children	children	children's
Personal pronouns				
SINGULAR	First person	I	me	mine
	Second person	you	you	your, yours
	Third person	he	him	his
		she	her	hers
		it	it	its
PLURAL	First person	we	us	our, ours
	Second person	you	you	your, yours
	Third person	they	them	their, theirs
Relative and interrogative pronouns				
SINGULAR, PLURAL		who	whom	whose
		whoever	whomever	—
		which, that, what	which, that, what	—
Indefinite pronouns				
		somebody	somebody	somebody's

Note: pronouns in the possessive case do not take an apostrophe:

Write	Don't write
yours (singular and plural)	your's, yours'
hers	her's, hers'
his	his', his's
its	it's, its'
ours	our's, ours'
theirs	their's, theirs'

Nouns take apostrophes to indicate possession. An apostrophe is used in *it's* to indicate contraction or abbreviation from a longer form (*it is*) rather than possession — see the discussion on punctuation (p. 115).

COMPOUND STRUCTURES

Compound structures (those using the conjunctions *and*, *nor*, *but*, *or*) sometimes cause confusion where case is concerned. For example, which are the correct pronouns in the following sentences?

Her/she and me/I decided to do a joint presentation on the project. They congratulated her/she and me/I on our presentation.

The solution is straightforward enough. Rewrite each sentence as if only one person was involved, not two, and see how the variations sound.

Variation	Yes/no?
Her decided to do . . .	no
She decided to do . . .	yes
Me decided to do . . .	no
I decided to do . . .	yes
They congratulated she . . .	no
They congratulated her . . .	yes
They congratulated I . . .	no
They congratulated me . . .	yes

Having worked out what the constituent parts of the compound construction are, we can now simply put those parts together again:

> She and I decided to do a joint presentation on the project.
> They congratulated her and me on our presentation.

This approach can be used to determine indirect objects as well as direct objects:

> They gave her and me a salary rise (not *she* and *I*).

It can also be used when appositives are used:

> Those remaining, she and I, had to clean up the mess. (*She* and *I* rename the subject of the sentence, *Those*.)
> James spoke to her and me, the only ones remaining. (*Her* and *me* rename the object of the sentence, *ones*.)

WE/US AND NOUNS

A similar approach can be taken when the first person plural pronouns are used with nouns:

> We/us accountants deserve more money.
> The boss told we/us accountants that we wouldn't get another penny.

Variation	Yes/no?
Us deserve ...	no
We deserve ...	yes
The boss told we ...	no
The boss told us ...	yes

PREPOSITIONAL PHRASES AND LINKING VERBS

Prepositional phrases are those beginning with prepositions, such as *as*, *before*, *between*, *by*, *despite*, *for*, *from*, *near*, *on*, *to* and *up* (see pp. 22, 51). Because prepositional phrases have an object, pronouns which appear after a preposition in a phrase must be in objective case. (Note, however, the special case of dependent clauses after prepositions in the following examples.)

The presentation was given by James and *me* (not *I*).
The work load was divided up between *her* and *me* (not *she* and *I*).

Linking verbs, as we have already seen (p. 28), include forms of the verb *to be* (*is*, *am*, *was*, *were*, etc.), plus other verbs such as *smell*, *feel*, *appear* and *become*. Such verbs (also known as *copulative* verbs) serve to rename or describe a sentence subject by linking it with a noun or adjective in the predicate. Such a noun or adjective is known as a subject complement:

I was happy.
They became bored.

Any pronoun appearing after a linking verb will rename the subject, and thus must take subjective case:

The authors were *she* and *I* (not *her* and *me*).

WHO/WHOM

The relative and interrogative pronouns *who* and *whoever* are subjective case, and *whom* and *whomever* are objective case. Problems sometimes arise when these words occur in independent or subordinate clauses and in questions.

When such a pronoun occurs in an independent clause, for example, we have to look at the function of that pronoun *within the clause*, irrespective of the clause's function within the larger sentence. Consider, for example, these sentences:

Seek opinions from whoever/whomever has expertise.
It hasn't been decided who/whom they should promote.

Let's take the first sentence first. At first glance, it would appear that the dependent clause *whoever/whomever has expertise* is the object of the preposition *from* and therefore the objective case *whomever* would be correct. In fact, however, we have to look at the dependent clause by itself, and then we see that *whoever* is the subject of *has expertise*. The correct word is thus *whoever*, not *whomever*.

In the second sentence, it may not be immediately clear what is happening in the dependent clause *who/whom they should promote*. In situations like this, re-write the clause as a separate sentence, replacing the relative pronoun with a personal pronoun:

Variation	Yes/no?
They should promote she.	no
They should promote her.	yes

Because the objective case *her* sounds better, we know that the correct relative pronoun will be the objective case *whom*:

It hasn't been decided whom they should promote.

Confusion can also arise in questions. Consider for example the following questions:

Who/whom made the presentation?
Who/whom did they ask for?

Answer the questions, and listen for the correct answer:

Variation	Yes/no?
Her made the presentation.	no
She made the presentation.	yes
They asked for she.	no
They asked for her.	yes

We can now determine the correct usage in the sentences:

Who made the presentation? (subjective case)
Whom did they ask for? (objective case)

THAN/AS AND PRONOUNS

Comparative sentences can lead to confusion when *than* or *as* are followed by pronouns. Consider, for example, the sentences:

He liked her more than I.
He liked her more than me.

Do these sentences mean the same thing? No, they don't. The first sentence is a shortened version of *He liked her more than I liked her* — a statement about which person had the greater liking. *I* is obviously the subject of the second *liked*, and therefore takes subjective case.

The second sentence means that he preferred one person to another — and thus the objective case *me* is appropriate.

Correct any errors you find in the following document.

INTERNAL MEMORANDUM	
To: Irene Adler	Subject: Clone Power project
From: Miles Standish	Date: August 4, 1995

I'm authorising Melanie to work with you on the Clone
Power project.

I want you and she to evaluate the competitiveness of
them printer costings, as per the July proposal document.

Accounts are always trying to muscle in on these
projects, and claim that it's theirs' to deal with, but I don't
see it like that. Us general staff have great skills in these
areas.

Get costings from whomever you can contact in
companies apart from Clono Power. Give a copy of the
figures to Isabel Archer. She and I will analyse them on
Friday next.

Answers on p. 170.

PRONOUN REFERENCE

The following sentence is a very old but still amusing example of ambiguous sentence construction.

> I'll hold the nail, and when I nod my head, you hit it with the hammer.

Ambiguity or confusion arises because of unclear pronoun reference: what does the pronoun 'it' refer to — the nail or my head? Logic would suggest the former rather than the latter, but the world is full of illogical people, and the consequences of misunderstanding, in this case and in others, might be painful.

Pronouns, as we have seen (p. 17) are words that stand in the place of nouns and other pronouns.[20] They include these words:

Personal pronouns	I/my/mine/me, you/your/yours (singular and plural), he/his/him, she/her/hers, it/its, we/our/ours/us, they/their/theirs/them
Relative pronouns	who/whose/whom, whoever/whomever, which, that, what, whatever
Indefinite pronouns	all, any, anybody, anyone, anything, each, either, everybody, everyone, everything, neither, nobody, none, no-one, nothing, one, some, somebody, someone, something

The noun or pronoun that a pronoun refers to is known as the *antecedent* — literally, it goes before. Precision in using a pronoun means placing it close to an antecedent and ensuring it refers to only one antecedent. Additional precision is gained by ensuring that pronouns and antecedents agree in person and number (see p. 81).

Ensure **that a pronoun refers to one antecedent.**

Consider the sentence:

Mary said to Joanne that she could go early.

The pronoun *she* is ambiguous: is it Mary or Joanne who can go early? The problem can be solved in a number of ways. The sentence could be restated:

Mary said to Joanne that Mary could go early.
Mary said to Joanne that Joanne could go early.

We could place the antecedent in parenthesis:

Mary said to Joanne that she (Mary) could go early.
Mary said to Joanne that she (Joanne) could go early.

We could also remove ambiguity by using direct speech:

Mary said to Joanne, 'I can go early.'
Mary said to Joanne, 'You can go early.'

The parenthesis solution is not very elegant, and should be avoided wherever possible. Restatement of the antecedent or using direct speech are acceptable solutions to the ambiguity problem.

Ensure **that a pronoun is close to its antecedent.**

Let's take our sentence about nails and heads:

I'll hold the nail, and when I nod my head, you hit it with the hammer.

We can restructure this sentence in a number of ways to make our meaning clearer:

I'll hold the nail, and when I nod my head, you hit it (the nail) with the hammer.
I'll hold the nail, and you hit it with the hammer when I nod my head.
When I nod my head, hit the nail that I'm holding with a hammer.

The first, parenthetical solution, is not ideal. The third solution is not acceptable either, as it introduces a new ambiguity. The second solution is the best. We have moved the pronoun closer to its antecedent within the sentence.

Be careful of placement of pronouns in longer passages:

When the colour fax machine finally arrived, there was much excitement. People came from several floors away, and soon a crowd of people were in the room, chattering away. There was much speculation about colour trueness, running costs, and the idealness or otherwise of the location — between the computer terminal and the drink machine. Suddenly, it beeped.

There is a problem here with more than one possible antecedent, but there is also a problem with the distance between the pronoun and its real antecedent. In a long passage like this, it is better to restate the antecedent, either totally or in part:

Suddenly, the fax machine beeped.

Use *that*, *which*, *this* and *it* with care.

Pronouns can cause problems in referring to single words, but pronouns such as *which*, *that*, *this* and *it* are particularly prone to cause ambiguity in clauses or sentences.

Consider this sentence:

> I had to raise $20 to buy this birthday cake, which was hard.

We might resolve ambiguity here by renaming the antecedent:

> I had to raise $20 to buy this birthday cake, a task which was hard.

A slightly less effective way of resolving ambiguity is by changing ambiguous modifiers:

> I had to raise $20 to buy this birthday cake, which was difficult.

Consider the following example:

> The desks for the temporary staff will need to be repaired, and their computers will have to be here by next week. This is a very trying problem for us.

The reader or listener is unsure of whether this refers to a problem of furniture, of equipment, or both. A preferable version would be:

> The desks for the temporary staff will need to be repaired, and their computers will have to be here by next week. These equipment and furniture problems are very trying.

Ensure that antecedents are clearly stated.

An antecedent needs to be a definite noun or pronoun, rather than something implied in a possessive, a modifier, another noun or pronoun, or a phrase or clause.

Consider this:

> You say that an angry customer is not a problem, but I wouldn't want to try to defuse it.

It is referring to a noun — *anger* — that is only implied in a modifer — *angry*. Some recasting will be necessary:

> You say this customer's anger is not a problem, but I wouldn't want to try to defuse it.

Consider the following example also:

> She has described this before, but it wasn't circulated widely.

A noun like *report* is needed here to make the sentence less confusing:

> She has described this before in a report, but it wasn't circulated widely.
>
> She has described this before, but the report wasn't circulated widely.

Use *it*, *they* and *you* carefully.

It is fairly common to hear people say things like:

> *It* says here that you can't connect that wire to that plug.
> *They* say in the papers that it will be fine today.
> On Mars, *you* need a pressurised suit just to survive.

All these uses of pronouns are vague. The third sentence, involving *you*, obviously is not referring to the reader or listener in a real situation at all. Such pronoun reference will be adequate in speech, but writers need to be more precise. If we recast the sentences above, we can make them more precise:

> *The writers of this manual state* that you can't connect that wire to that plug.
> *The newspaper weather forecast predicts* that it will be fine today.
> On Mars, *humans* need pressurised suits just to survive.

Use *that*, *which* and *who* correctly.

Referring to people or things

Who is used to refer to people, but occasionally is used to refer to animals with names:

> Jonathan is the person *who* has all that information.
> Skippy the bush kangaroo is a television character *who* is popular in many countries.

That and *which* refer to things and animals, and sometimes to people viewed collectively or anomymously:

> The chair *which* collapsed is in the corner.
> The team *that* performed best this year got the prize.

Restrictive and non-restrictive clauses

Choice of pronouns can also be affected by the question of whether the clauses they appear in are restrictive or non-restrictive (see p. 108). *That* is used in restrictive clauses, or those clauses which are integral to the sentence's meaning, and which therefore cannot be dropped without making the sentence meaningless. *Which* is used in non-restrictive clauses, or those clauses which are not integral to the sentence's meaning, and which therefore can be dropped without making the sentence meaningless:

> Computers *that are sold cheap* tend to be slow. (Restrictive: *that* introduces vital information about the sentence subject.)
> Computers, *which are seen in most workplaces now*, tend to be slow if they are cheap. (Non-restrictive: *which* introduces information that could be deleted without damaging the sentence or distorting its meaning.)

EXERCISE 6.1:

PRONOUN REFERENCE

Correct any errors you find in the document below.

CLONE POWER

MEMORANDUM

To: George Shaw
From: Priscilla Khan
Subject: Reconditioned machine sales
Date: 24 June, 1994

I think you should talk to our dealers about our reconditioned machines. I think we have a problem with them. Pete was talking to Irving Miller of the South Street shop, and he wasn't happy after the conversation. He said that the profit margin on a reconditioned machine was just too low compared to which of a new machine, and that it just wasn't good enough. He's the kind of person who doesn't know much about customer psychology, which Pete hasn't yet understood.

What the dealers don't seem to understand is that our research shows that they tend to buy the more expensive machines after they have become uncomfortable with their limitations. It was done specifically for our marketing department, so it's no wonder that they don't understand it. Yet when I was in retailing, you knew these things as a matter of course. They say that customers won't lay out cash on more elaborate systems or even upgrade their reconditioned systems, but this does happen. I know it happens.

Answers on p. 171.

7

AGREEMENT

Person (first, second, third), number (singular, plural) and gender (male, female) are important aspects of the variations in some parts of speech. Let's turn our attention now to the ways in which verbs agree in number and person with their subjects, and the ways in which pronouns agree in number, person and gender with their antecedents.

SUBJECT–VERB AGREEMENT

Nouns which form their plurals in a regular way do so by the simple addition of *-s* or *-es*. Exceptions to this rule are nouns which form their plurals by means of internal changes (*woman/women, ox/oxen*) and nouns which have the same form for singular and plural (*sheep/sheep, deer/deer*).

Verbs in the present tense form their third person singular forms by adding *-s* or *-es*.

> The girl run*s*.
> The girl*s* run.
> The actress teach*es* her understudy.
> The actress*es* teach their understudies.

Ensure words between subject and verb do not distract.

Words and word groups, such as prepositional phrases, can distract the eye and the ear when we are trying to ensure agreement between subject and verb:

> A box of apples, oranges, peaches, pears and plums *were* on the driveway. ☒

There is only one box (subject), irrespective of how many objects it contains, so the verb must be singular.

> A box of apples, oranges, peaches, pears and plums *was* on the driveway. ☑
> The nineteen players, together with their charismatic captain, *was* in training. ☒

The real subject (players) is plural, and so the verb must be plural.

> The nineteen players, together with their charismatic captain, *were* in training. ☑

Use plural verbs with subjects connected by *and*.

When two or more subjects are joined by the conjunction *and*, they comprise a compound subject and, as such, take a plural verb:

The Arabs *and* Israelis are seeking a new agreement.
Rock and roll *and* rhythm and blues are two contemporary musical forms.

Exception: if modifiers such as *each* and *every* precede singular subjects within a compound subject, use singular verbs:

Every man, woman and child *was* saved.
Each ice crystal and water droplet *evaporates* in the sunshine.

If *each* follows a compound subject, however, a plural verb is appropriate:

Maria and Justine each *hope* to win the prize.

Ensure that in compound subjects the verb agrees with the subject closest to it.

The correlative conjunctions (see p. 24) are:

both ... and
whether ... or
either ... or
neither ... nor
not only ... but (also)

When subjects are linked by one of the latter three coordinate conjunctions, or by *or* or *nor*, then the verb should agree with the subject closest to it:

Neither rain nor storms *stop* our postal service.
Not only his fans but also his manager *believes* he can do it.

While the last sentence pattern (plural subject + singular subject + singular verb) is technically correct, it may grate on the ear and eye. In situations like this, it is better to recast the sentence so that the plural subject comes last:

Not only his manager but also his fans believe he can do it.

Use singular verbs for most indefinite pronouns.

The indefinite pronouns are:

all	either	neither	one
anybody	everybody	nobody	some
anyone	everyone	none	somebody
anything	everything	no-one	someone
each	more	nothing	something

By definition, such pronouns[21] do not refer to specific individuals or things. Generally, indefinite pronouns take a singular verb:

> Everybody *is* welcome.
> Nobody *has* been there for a long time.
> Anything *goes*.

Several indefinite pronouns (*all, any, more, most, none* and *some*) take either a singular or a plural verb, depending upon the particular sentence:

> Some of the tenpins *were* still standing. (*Some* refers to a plural — *tenpins*.)
> Some of this dessert *is* left. (*Some* refers to a singular — *dessert*.)
> Some seats are gone, but more *are* available. (*More* refers to a plural — *seats*.)
> More of that argument *gets* us nowhere. (*More* refers to a singular — *argument*.)

Ensure **the correct use of singular or plural verbs with collective nouns.**

A collective noun behaves like a singular noun, even though it is describing a collectivity — *family, team, herd, staff, committee, crowd, congregation*. When it is the subject in a sentence, a collective noun will take a singular verb when the members of the collectivity behave collectively, and will take a plural verb when the members of the collectivity behave individually:

> The team *is* united on this issue
> The team *are* having their photos taken.

Note: even though the collective noun + plural verb combination is correct in some situations, it can grate on the eye and ear. If this is the case, recast the sentence so that a more obvious plural subject appears:

> The members of the team *are* having their photos taken.

Ensure **that certain plural subjects take singular verbs.**

Certain nouns with *-s* endings are usually regarded as singular: *news, mathematics, physics, statistics, economics,* and *measles.*

> Here *is* the news.
> Mathematics *is* very difficult for some.

Certain quantities — money, distance, measurement — are also regarded as singular:

> Five dollars *is* just too much for that.
> Forty kilometres *is* a long way to run, but that is just what marathon runners do.

However, plural verbs are appropriate when these quantities or nouns with *-s* endings refer to particular, rather than general things:

> The road fatality statistics from the different states *are* alarming.
> Forty per cent of the staff *have* not been photographed.

Ensure **that titles take singular verbs.**

> Titles of artistic works and organisations, and words referred to as words must take a singular verb.

> > *Crime and Punishment is* my favourite piece of light reading.
> > Procter and Gamble *is* a large transnational corporation.
> > 'The disappeared' *is* a term used to describe people in some Latin American countries who have been abducted by — and probably murdered by — secret police forces.

PRONOUN–ANTECEDENT AGREEMENT

> As we saw in the previous chapter, pronoun reference to antecedents can be a complex affair. We now take this analysis further, and look at the way in which pronouns should agree in person (first, second and third), number (singular, plural) and gender (masculine, feminine, neuter).

Ensure **pronouns and antecedents agree in person, number and gender.**

> The antecedent is the noun or pronoun to which a pronoun refers:

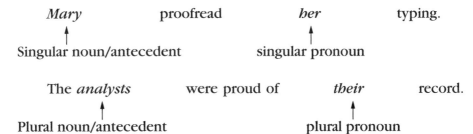

Ensure **the correct use of pronouns with antecedents joined by *and*.**

> When two or more antecedents are joined by *and* (that is, comprise a compound antecedent), they take a plural pronoun, even if the antecedents are singular:

> > Bonnie and Clyde met *their* end in an ambush.
> > Egypt and Israel had a long negotiating session before *them*.

> When a compound antecedent is preceded by *each* or *every*, however, the pronoun is singular:

> > Each boy and man in the group had to sing *his* part without rehearsal.

Ensure **that in compound antecedents the pronoun agrees with the closest antecedent.**

> We saw with verb–subject agreement (p. 78) that in sentences containing certain conjunctions, it is the last subject that determines the verb. A similar pattern prevails with pronouns and antecedents — that

is, the pronoun will agree with the number and person of the last antecedent:

> Neither the computer nor the software packages have had *their* prices checked.
>
> Neither the software packages nor the computer has had *its* price checked.

Although the second sentence pattern (plural antecedent + singular antecedent + singular pronoun) is technically correct, it may grate on the ear and eye. In situations like this, it is better to recast the sentence so that the plural antecedent comes last, as in the first sentence.

Use singular pronouns for most indefinite pronoun antecedents.

As we have seen with subject–verb agreement (p. 78), most indefinite pronouns behave like singular nouns. A similar pattern prevails with pronouns and antecedents:

> Everybody should consider *his or her* position before signing the agreement.
>
> Each of the girls was determined to keep *her* place on the team.

Note, however:

> All of the girls were determined to keep *their* places on the team.

Ensure you avoid using sexist pronouns.

Traditionally, the masculine pronouns *he*, *his* and *him* were used to refer to both females and males:

> Everyone should consider *his* position before signing the agreement.
>
> The average worker has much industrial change before *him*, and will have much to consider if *he* wishes to retain *his* traditional wage level.

Society has moved on since those times, and now it is sound practice to acknowledge females as well as males in pronoun constructions. There are a number of ways in which this can be done, some less satisfactory than others:

• Use both masculine and feminine pronouns, linked by or:

> Each worker should check *his or her* salary slip for mistakes.

• Use masculine and feminine pronouns, linked by a slash:

> Each worker should check *his/her* salary slip for mistakes.
> *S/he* may find such attention necessary.

• Revise the sentence, creating a plural antecedent and pronoun:

> All workers should check *their* salary slips for mistakes.

• Recast the sentence to avoid pronouns altogether:

> Salary slips should be checked for mistakes by all workers.

Ensure **the correct use of pronouns with collective noun antecedents.**

As we saw with subject-verb agreement (p. 78), collective nouns behave like singulars or plurals, depending upon the situation. A similar pattern prevails with noun antecedents and their pronouns:

The team is united on this issue, and not likely to change *its* mind.

Here, the group is acting together as a group, rather than separately as individuals, so the singular pronoun is appropriate.

The team are having *their* identification photos taken.

Here, the members of the group are acting as individuals, rather than together as a group, so the plural pronoun is appropriate.

EXERCISE 7.1:

AGREEMENT

Correct any errors you find in the document below. If necessary, recast sentences to clarify meaning.

JUGGERNAUT
MANUFACTURING, Inc

INTERNAL MEMORANDUM	
To: Irene Adler	Subject: R & D/ Team B
From: Satoshi Sakamoto	Date: 29 April, 1995

The Research and Development Department are giving us a hard time on gathering data from our experimental assembly team, Team B. Can you please intervene? They and their supervisor, Brian Maddox, thinks we've got it easy here, but that is not so. We're having trouble organising the data: we're collating data from more than one project, and so far it is proving to be contradictory. Brian doesn't seem to understand this, and isn't happy even when we give him these data. Statistics are what he majored in in his degree, but it's a pity he can't understand what these statistics is saying.

We are also having trouble with the team, data or no data. The team agree that efficiency has to be improved in all three areas, but these are slow in happening. I've put a new member (Belinda Hawkins) on the team, and I hope that this make a difference. Each of the members of the team has to accept their responsibility from now on. The typical team member has to see that pay and job security is what he chooses to make it.

Possible answers on p. 172.

8

MORE ON ADJECTIVES AND ADVERBS

We looked at adjectives and adverbs earlier when we were considering the parts of speech; now it is time to give them some closer attention.

Adjectives and adverbs do quite separate jobs, and they should not be confused. Firstly, they modify different parts of speech and constructions.

Adjectives modify:	nouns	*bad* man
	pronouns	He was *bad*.
Adverbs modify:	verbs	drives *badly*
	adverbs	*extremely* quickly
	adjectives	*very* happy
	phrases	*almost* off the roof
	clauses	*precisely* where she landed
	sentences	*Naturally*, I'll be there.

Adjectives and adverbs also answer different questions.

Adjectives answer these questions:	• What kind? • Which one? • How many? • Whose?
Adverbs answer these questions:	• Where? • When? • How? • How often? • To what extent or degree?

Many adverbs are formed by adding *-ly* to adjectives, although this is not a foolproof way of identifying adverbs: some adverbs do not have *-ly* endings, and some adjectives do (see table 8.1). It all depends upon the task any given word is performing — that is, what part of speech or construction is it modifying, and what question is it answering? In fact, as we have seen earlier (p.11), a number of words — for example, *round*, *that*, *over* — can be both adjectives and adverbs, depending upon their role in a sentence.

Table 8.1: Examples of adjectives and adverbs with different endings

	-ly endings	Non-*-ly* endings
Adjectives	lovely, lonely, ghastly, friendly, motherly	quick, slow, loud, notorious, bad, fast
Adverbs	quickly, slowly, loudly, notoriously, badly	around, up, often, there, fast

Ensure **you don't confuse adjectives and adverbs.**

Remember the functions of the two different parts of speech, and ensure that you don't confuse them. Such confusions happen often enough, particularly in spoken rather than written language:

He spoke *real proper*. ☒

He spoke *really* (or *quite*) *properly*. ☑

That drink goes down *easy*. ☒

That drink goes down *easily*. ☑

The adjective *bad* and adverb *badly* are often confused.

I feel *badly* about the way I treated her. ☒

I feel *bad* about the way I treated her. ☑

Since I damaged my fingertips with that grinder, I feel *bad*. ☒

Since I damaged my fingertips with that grinder, I feel *badly*. ☑

Bad describes the nature of an emotion; badly describes the effectiveness of the sense of touch. In spite of this, many people feel uncomfortable with saying *I feel bad* (for example, about what I've done) because, to their ears, it sounds improper.

The adjective *good* and the adverb *well* are also often confused.

He dances *good*. ☒

He dances *well*. ☑

Note: *well* can be an adjective when referring to health, but in all other contexts it is an adverb.

Use **correct comparative and superlative forms.**

Adjectives and adverbs are particularly useful when comparing the quantity or quality of people, animals or things. Table 8.2 gives us a framework for making such comparisons.

When no comparisons are being made, the adjective or adverb used is said to be in its *positive* form. When two things are being compared, the adjective or adverb being used is known as the *comparative*. When three or more things are being compared, the adjective or adverb being used is known as the *superlative*. Just to complicate matters, comparisons can be negative, showing a diminution of quality or quantity. When two things are being negatively compared, the adjective or adverb being used is known as the *negative comparative*. When three or more things are being negatively compared, the adjective or adverb being used is known as the *negative superlative*.

Generally speaking, adjectives and adverbs of one syllable form their comparative forms by adding -*er*, and form their superlative forms by adding -*est*. With most adverbs of two or more syllables, the comparative is formed by adding the prefix word *more*, while the superlative is formed using *most*. With some adjectives of two syllables, the -*er*/-*est* is the system used, while for others, the *more/most* system is used. Indeed, some two-syllable adjectives (*lazy, fancy, steady*) can take either system. If unsure which system prevails for a particular adjective, consult a dictionary (see p. 134). For adjectives of three or more syllables, use the *more/most* system.

Table 8.2: Forms of adverbs and adjectives

Negative superlative	Negative comparative	Positive	Comparative	Superlative
least white	less white	white	whiter	whitest
least effective	less effective	effective	more effective	most effective
least near	less near	near	nearer	nearest
least quickly	less quickly	quickly	more quickly	most quickly
		many, much, some	more	most
		good, well	better	best
worst	worse	bad, badly		
least	less	little		

Certain adjectives and adverbs (*bad, badly, many, much, some, good, well, little*) take comparative and superlative forms in irregular ways.

The comparative forms are used when two things are being compared:

> She was the *better* of the two women swimmers.
> If we are considering general analytical skills of the two candidates, he is clearly the *less talented*.

The superlative forms are used when three or more things are being compared:

> It was the *best* thing I had ever seen.
> He was the *least capable* student in the class.

The *-er/-est* and *more/most* systems should never be combined, because that would create redundant expressions:

> He was the *more quicker* of the two. ☒
>
> He is the *quicker* of the two. ☑
>
> He was the *most biggest* person I had ever seen. ☒
>
> He was the *biggest* person I had ever seen. ☑

For further information on redundant expressions, see p. 88.

Note also that some things are absolute in condition, and cannot be modified by *more* or *most*:

perfect	dead
round	empty
central	unique
straight	impossible
favourite	infinite

Modifiers like *nearly* or *almost* can be used with these, however.

Note also that *less* and *fewer* do not mean the same thing. *Less* modifies mass nouns, and *fewer* modifies count nouns (p. 15):

> We need *fewer* bricks and *less* mortar for this job.

Avoid **double negatives.**

A double-negative construction is one where two negative modifiers are used: either one is redundant, or one cancels the other out, making the statement a positive one (which is probably not what the writer or speaker wished to convey):

> Although the rain was falling, I *never* felt *nothing*. ☒
>
> Although the rain was falling hard, I never felt anything. ☑
>
> Although the rain was falling hard, I felt nothing. ☑

Avoid using series of nouns as modifiers.

Nouns are used fairly commonly to modify other nouns:

truck driver   telephone call   light bulb   computer printout

Confusion rarely arises with such simple instances. Confusion may arise, however, when a series of nouns are linked together, and the reader or listener is simply not clear on the question of just which word is modifying which:

government environment region planning survey
hospital administration staff redeployment budgets report

In the first phrase, what is the survey about, and whom is it conducted by? Is it conducted by a government or a region? Is it about the environment, or a government environment? Similar confusion prevails in the second sentence. The only thing we can be sure of is that we are dealing with a report.

When confronted with too many noun modifiers, recast the words to bring out meaning, using possessive case, converting nouns to adjectives, or converting nouns to phrases. Recast versions (by no means the only ones) of the above phrases are:

the government's survey of environmental planning at the regional level

a report on budgets for redeployment activities written by staff in hospital administration

These versions are longer than the originals, but there is no point in brevity if it introduces ambiguity.

Avoid redundant modifiers.

Adjectives and adverbs are often unnecessary in some constructions, but people use them anyway, perhaps in an attempt to emphasise the point they are trying to make, or because they are using them as conversational spacers (to give themselves time to think) or else because they simply haven't thought about it. Such modifiers are redundant, and are known as tautologies. Some examples are:

repeat back	true facts
repeat again	back back (of a vehicle)
separate out	advance forward
false illusion	past history
basic fundamentals	combine together
surrounding circumstances	completely full
consensus of opinion	my own personal opinion
circle around	might possibly
close proximity	still remains
absolutely essential	big, enormous . . .
new initiatives	sufficient enough
forward planning	circular in shape

Redundant modifiers are absurd, but we shouldn't make too much of a fuss about them if people use only one or two. Problems may arise, however, if a writer or speaker uses them continually. Like clichés, they can be an indicator of flabby thinking. The test for redundant modifiers is the reversal test: can you have false facts, old initiatives, real illusions? Can you circle in a square? Such a test can be a useful way of identifying genuine redundant modifiers, and it can also be useful to evaluate just how effective (apparently) more legitimate modifiers are. For example, if I accuse you of *irresponsible opportunism* and *crass ignorance*, you might apply the reversal test and ask me what might *responsible opportunism* and *refined ignorance* look like. Perhaps what people mean when they use modifers in this way is better expressed by a noun plus noun combination rather than a modifer plus noun combination: *irresponsibility and opportunism* and *crassness and ignorance*, for example. Such inexactness — not really thinking about the meanings of the modifying words and the words which are purportedly being modified — can also be seen in double negative constructions (*badly mismanaged company*).

Use sentence modifiers or disjuncts with care.

Some adverbs modify entire sentences:

> *Naturally*, I'll be there.
> *Regrettably*, she couldn't come.

Such sentence modifiers are also known as disjuncts. Fashions come and go in usage of the language, and some observers have noted that disjuncts are being used more often in recent years. While such observers have noted the change, they have not always noted it with pleasure, seeing in some disjuncts the same behavioural pattern of dishonesty and evasion that is sometimes seen in the use of the passive voice (see p. 42).

For example, controversy has arisen in recent years about one disjunct in particular, *hopefully*, although there has been similar controversy about others such as *arguably, interestingly, reportedly* and *presumably*.

The traditional meaning of hopefully is as a normal modifier:

> She waited *hopefully* (i.e., with hope) for them to arrive.

The newer, more controversial usage is that of a disjunct:

> *Hopefully* (i.e., it is hoped), they will arrive soon.

Critics of this usage include the novelist Kingsley Amis, who argues that the person who uses the word in this way:

> . . . can't say 'I hope' because that would imply that he has surrendered control of events; he can't really use J. F. Kennedy's favourite, 'I am hopeful that,' without being J. F. Kennedy; he can't say 'with luck' which is all he means; so he says 'hopefully' and basks in a fraudulent glow of confidence.[22]

Others believe that no psychological games are being played, and that *hopefully* is as legitimate as *naturally, regrettably*, and so on.[23]

People who comment on language usage tend to be either prescriptivists — those who believe that rules are rules, and that certain usage is not acceptable, even if widespread — or descriptivists — those who believe that if usage is widespread, then that is what language is. Thus, Amis is a prescriptivist on *hopefully*, and his opponents are descriptivists, accepting the widespread use of the newer meaning. I (the writer of this book) tend to side with prescriptivists on this one. I think that most people use the word as code for 'I don't have much hope at all — go away and don't bother me', or 'possibly', or 'with luck'. When I hear people use the word, I tend to also see various non-verbal accompaniments — a shrug, raised eyebrows, appealing/despairing palm displays, and a breaking of eye contact. I see the newer meaning of *hopefully* as being a mind-game, where a person seems to offer hope, but simultaneously withdraws it.

I don't believe that it is as harmless as other disjuncts or sentence modifiers, because virtually all of those — *thankfully, luckily, happily* — usually relate to events in the past, and therefore events about which one doesn't have to do anything. *Hopefully*, in contrast, usually relates to events in the future, and therefore to events which one might be able to act on or influence. The *hopefully* user, however, doesn't want to act — that's the whole point.

As mentioned earlier, behavioural games played with disjuncts may be similar to behavioural games played with passive voice constructions, which can sometimes be word-games signalling evasiveness and avoidance of responsibility. This disjunct-plus passive combination can be a powerful one, but its message may not be clear until you challenge it.

Consider, for example, a situation in which you are about to be operated on, and you can choose your surgeon. Surgeon 1 says, 'Hopefully, you'll pull through'. Surgeon 2 says, 'I hope to pull you through'. Consider another situation, where you are talking to someone at a counter about a lost parcel. Salesperson 1 says, 'Hopefully, your parcel will be found'. Salesperson 2 says, 'I hope to find your parcel'. I would choose surgeon 2 and salesperson 2 because they sound committed.

As with passive voice, it is always wise with disjuncts to apply the owl test: ask *Whoooo?*[24] Who is hopeful? Who is arguing? Who is presuming? Who is reporting? Who is interested? Usually the answer is, no-one at all — but it sounds good to say it like this.[25] As we saw with the passive voice, the confrontation and honesty implicit in the active voice — 'I have lost your parcel.' — can be weakened by switching into the passive — 'Your parcel has been lost by me.' — and then eliminated altogether by using the impersonal passive — 'Your parcel has been lost.' No human agency or responsibility exists in the world of the last sentence — events just happen mysteriously. The disappearing person trick seems to follow a pre-set grammatical sequence:

OPEN COMMUNICATION ———→ → → → CLOSED COMMUNICATION				
Stage 1	**Stage 2**	**Stage 3**	**Stage 4**	**Stage 5**
First person singular	**First person plural**	**Third person**	**Impersonal passive**	**Disjunct**
I regret	We regret	The company regrets	It is regretted	Regrettably
I hope	We hope	The government hopes	It is hoped	Hopefully

This is a sequence beloved of bureaucrats the world over, and one all too familiar to the hapless readers and listeners who have to deal with such bureaucrats. If you find yourself being pushed from the left to the right of the continuum in communicating with others, retaliate by asking the owl question — whoooo? If you find that your own style of communication is more to the right rather than to the left of the continuum, it might be wise to start considering your motives, or, if you work in an organisation, at least to start analysing the organisational culture that permits and encourages such communication.

The newer sense of *hopefully* also makes it that much easier for ambiguity to sneak into the language. For example, it's particularly prone to end up being a squinting modifier (p. 98):

Our team will start their innings hopefully immediately after tea.

Does the modifier tell us about the team's manner, or our expectations? It's just not clear.[26]

If you feel the need to use the newer meaning of *hopefully*, but are reasonably committed to the ideal of more honest and less ambiguous human communication, I would suggest this decision rule to you:

4. Do you have a lot of hope about a situation, and can you back up that hope with action?
   If so, use *I hope*.
5. Do you have little hope about a situation, and will not or cannot do anything about it?
   If so, use *possibly* or *with luck*.

The usage tip with disjuncts, then, as with passive voice, is to use sparingly, and be alert to extra-grammatical meanings which might be being deployed — consciously or unconsciously — by yourself or others.

Of course, this might all be a storm in a teacup. It's up to you to determine whether disjunctive modifiers are a barrier to effective communication, or whether they are merely a convenient short-cut, with no sinister hidden meanings, and therefore in fact an aid to effective communication. What do you think?

EXERCISE 8.1:

INEFFECTIVE MODIFIERS

Correct any misuse of modifiers in the following passage.

JUGGERNAUT

MANUFACTURING, Inc

1000 Eastmore Road, Newtown 68113 Freedonia

Telephone (61.2) 419.6911 • Toll-free (61) 008.420.4322
• Facsimile (61.2) 419.6924 • Telex (61.2) 54437 JUGGER.

Dr A. K. Jones,   29 June, 1995
Managing Director,
AKJ Components Ltd.,
416 Terraform Boulevard,
Outremer 61213

Dear Dr Jones:
Thank you for letter of 16 June.
I was extreme impressed by your machines test-bed
performance data comparison report on your AKJ-10 and the
Visigoth brand B-6 machine we have been successful using on
our assembly lines. If your numerical data is correct, then
clearly the AKJ-10 is definitely the most goodest of the pair of
two machines. We may have a totally unique opportunity here
to do business, but we will need to proceed along careful.

My own personal opinion is that we need to test out some
new innovations in this field real quick, so long as any basic
fundamentals we seem to discover are not a false illusion. Any
true facts that emerged from such a thoroughly procedure
would provide sufficient enough justification to continue on to
explore the more than infinite possibilities of the AKJ-10.
Arguably, any forwardest planning would then be based upon
such whatever valuable data that was gathered, and hopefully
there would never be no need to return back to the old
technology of yesterday. Interestingly, the entire whole B-6
assembly line mechanism has been producing less errors in
the past week, and if it continues on to perform good, then my
superiors would be less likely inclined to consider thinking
about the type of total perfection of your AKJ-10 when they
can have another least perfect alternative option. Please ring,
and we'll continue on to talk further about this.

Regards,

Irene Adler

Irene Adler.

Suggested solution on p. 173.

9

SHIFTS AND MISUSED MODIFIERS

Faults in sentence construction can cause considerable ambiguity and confusion. Among the most common faults are those of inappropriate shifts in person and number, tense and mood, subject and voice, and direct and indirect quotation. Words, phrases or clauses which modify other words, phrases or clauses can also distort meaning if not handled correctly.

SHIFTS

Avoid **shifts in person and number.**

Number and person refer to specific communication relationships.

	First person (shows person speaking or writing)	Second person (shows person being spoken or written to)	Third person (shows person or thing written about)
Singular	I, me, mine, etc.	You, yourself, etc.	He, she, it, hers, the accountant, etc.
Plural	We, our, us, etc.	You, yours, etc.	They, them-selves, the accountants, etc.

The picture is complicated somewhat by the indefinite pronouns, *one*, *you* and *they*. These tend to be used to describe people in general:

One should be there if *one* wants to be involved.
You have to drive on the left in this country.
They say that the sun will eventually cool down.

It is best to classify the indefinite *you* as second person and the indefinite *they* as third person. *One* is third person, even though at times it sounds like first person (and even second person).

Shift errors occur when the writer or speaker makes improper shifts in person or point of view:

If *you* go there, a *person* could get hurt. ☒

If *you* go there, *you* could get hurt. ☑

If *a person/one/he/she/he* or *she* goes there, *a person/one/he/she/he* or *she* could get hurt. ☑

When *a person* goes to a restaurant like that, *you* expect better service. ☒

When a person goes to a restaurant like that, *a person/one/he/she/he* or *she* expects better service. ☑

I really like it when *you* go into a shop and there is music playing. ☒

I really like it when *I* go into a shop and there is music playing. ☑

Similar types of shift error occur when the writer or speaker misuses number:

Although *everyone* is meant to be able to fill in these forms, *a student* could still find them confusing. ☒

Although *everyone* is meant to be able to fill in these forms, *students* could still find them confusing. ☑

Avoid shifts in subject and voice.

When we create a sentence in the active voice (p. 42), the subject names the actor (the person or thing doing something):

John *opened* the suitcase.

When we create a sentence in the passive voice, the subject names the receiver of the action:

The suitcase *was opened* by John.

Occasionally, we will shift voice within a sentence because it helps the meaning of that sentence:

They *lived* without incident on the farm for three years, but then *were abducted* that night in June.

Such a construction reinforces the notion that the subject of the first clause did not disappear because of their own actions, as the subject of the second clause is unknown. The focus thus remains on the subject we want the reader or listener to focus upon.

When we shift subject and voice in other sentences, however, it can distract because of the introduction of other subjects and/or the creation of ambiguities about just who is doing what to whom:

When they installed that new screen, its low-radiation surface must have been damaged by them. ☒

When they installed that new screen, they must have damaged its low-radiation surface. ☑

I opened the door and he was thrown out. ☒

I opened the door and threw him out. ☑

Avoid shifts in tense.

Tense is the way we convey meanings about time (see p. 37). Tense shifts are sometimes necessary to convey the meaning of a sentence or a group of sentences.

Although we *have had* our differences in the past, the relationship *is* now better, and we *will* undoubtedly *have* a very productive relationship in the future.

Nevertheless, some tense shifts are invalid, and can be quite confusing to the reader or listener:

The burglar climbed up the ladder and then *smashes* a window. ☒

The burglar climbed up the ladder and then *smashed* a window. ☑

Hamlet *seems to become* more decisive in the next act, but then he *became* depressed again. ☒

Hamlet *seems to become* more decisive in the next act, but then he *becomes* depressed again. ☑

Avoid shifts in mood.

The intentions of the writer or speaker can be conveyed through mood (p. 42). There are three moods:

Indicative: I typed the letter.
Imperative: Type that letter now.
Subjunctive: If I were you, I would type that letter now.

Clumsiness or ambiguity can arise when shifts in mood occur:

Connect the printer cable to the back of the computer, and then you *should turn* the printer on. (Shift from imperative to indicative mood). ☒

Connect the printer cable to the back of the computer, and then *turn* the printer on. ☑

You *should connect* the printer cable to the back of the computer, and you *should* then *turn* the computer on. ☑

If you were to buy at that particular price, the *guarantee* is still valid. (Shift from subjunctive to indicative). ☒

If you were to buy at that particular price, the *guarantee would be* still valid. ☑

Avoid **unnecessary shifts between direct and indirect quotation.**

Direct quotation is used to reproduce the exact words of a speaker:

'I'm just not getting the productivity out of these machines that I expected,' Maria observed.

Indirect quotation is used when the actual words of a person are being reported, but not necessarily word for word:

Maria said that she was just not getting the productivity out of those machines that she expected.

Shifting carelessly between one style and another can create confused and clumsy sentences:

Maria said that she had had to install the machines herself and 'Now I'm just not getting the productivity out of them that I expected.' ☒

Maria said that she had had to install the machines herself and now was just not getting the productivity out of them that she expected. ☑

Maria said, 'I have had to install these machines myself, and now I am just not getting the productivity out of them that I expected.' ☑

MODIFIERS

Avoid **misplaced modifiers.**

Words, phrases and clauses can modify the meaning of other words, phrases and clauses (see p. 50 and p. 53 for information on phrases and clauses). Sometimes this can cause unintentionally humorous effects, and sometimes it just causes plain confusion and ambiguity.

Ensure you place modifiers carefully.

Limiting modifiers (*only, scarcely, just, hardly, almost, even*) need to be positioned carefully. Consider for example the variations in meaning in the following sentences merely by changing the position of the word *only*:

> *Only* I walked down the road.
> I *only* walked down the road.
> I walked *only* down the road.
> I walked down the *only* road.
> I walked down the road *only*.

Careful placement is needed also with modifiers such as *other* and *another*. It is fairly common, for example, to see and hear sentences like these:

> He was replaced by another woman.
> I met her and four other men.
> We will undertake liaison with industry and other vocational schools.

The adjectives *other/another* here fall between nouns or pronouns (or modified nouns): *He/woman, her/men, industry/vocational schools*. Clarity would be better served in these sentences if the adjectives *other/another* were to modify generic nouns:

> He was replaced by another *person*.
> I met her and four other *people*.
> We will undertake liaison with industry and other *groups/interested parties*, etc.

The speakers or writers of our ambiguous sentences, however, usually wish to emphasise specific, not generic nouns — in which case they should drop the adjectives altogether.

Ambiguity can also occur when adjectives are placed so as to modify more than one word. A sentence like the following is clear enough:

> I was criticised by angry friends and relatives.

It is reasonable to assume that both friends and relatives are angry. But what about sentences like these?

> I was surrounded by barking dogs and cats.
> We flew over frozen tundra and lakes.

In both of these sentences, it is just not clear as to where the modifier stops modifying. To remove ambiguity, we need to either insert other, specific modifiers (*yowling/spitting* cats, *tranquil/choppy/melting/unfrozen* lakes), or else to recast the sentences, so that the modifier only modifies what it is meant to be modifying:

> I was surrounded by cats and barking dogs.
> We flew over lakes and frozen tundra.

Avoid **squinting modifiers.**

A squinting modifier creates ambiguity by having the potential to modify what precedes it as well as what comes after it:

> The people who were renting the house *temporarily* vacated it.

Does this mean that the people who were renting on a temporary basis have now vacated, or does it mean that the people who were renting for an unspecified period have temporarily vacated? It's just not clear. When modifiers squint to the left and to the right, we don't see things all that clearly either. Some sentence modification is called for. (Here, the placement of 'have' on either side of the modifier would remove ambiguity.)

Avoid **dangling modifiers.**

A dangling modifier is a phrase or clause that causes ambiguity because the word which should be modified is not present, or is only there by implication. Dangling modifiers usually occur in prepositional phrases, participial phrases, infinitive phrases (see p. 51) and elliptical clauses (see p. 56). Let's consider some examples in table 9.1.

Table 9.1: Examples of dangling modifiers

Dangling modifier	Example	Ambiguity
Prepositional phrase	*After eating our meal*, the horses were saddled.	Who/what eats?
Infinitive phrase	*To win that contest*, talent will need to combine with relentless training.	Who/what wins?
Participial phrase	*Running into the street*, the bus narrowly missed me. *Obviously intoxicated*, we helped him to his feet.	Who/what misses? Who is intoxicated?
Elliptical clause	*While still a child*, my mother would walk me to school.	Who is a child?

All of these modifiers precede the independent clause in their respective sentences. The subject is unclear, with part of the problem being the use of the passive voice. Ambiguities can be resolved by a number of means — inserting a subject, inserting a subject and verb, and/or converting passive voice construction to active voice construction:

- After eating our meal, we saddled our horses./When we ate our meal, the horses were saddled.

- To win that contest, you will need to combine talent with relentless training./If you are to win that contest, talent will need to combine with relentless training.
- Running into the street, I was narrowly missed by a bus./As I was running into the street, the bus narrowly missed me.
- Obviously intoxicated, he needed to be helped to his feet by us./As he was obviously intoxicated, we helped him to his feet.
- While I was still a child, my mother would walk me to school./While still a child, I was walked to school by my mother.

Ensure you minimise use of split infinitives.

For many users of English, the split infinitive is one of the cardinal sins, although the revulsion they feel at its contemplation is usually unfounded. The infinitive is the *to-* form of a verb: *to go, to think, to be*. To split an infinitive is to put one or more modifiers between the *to-* and the verb:

> To *further* complicate matters, she arrived soon after.
> I want you to *completely, unflinchingly and vigorously* eliminate these pests.
> I will tell her to *not* go.

Split infinitives rarely result in ambiguities, but they can make your sentences sound clumsy. In some sentences, however, it may be better to leave the infinitive split rather than create a clumsy rhythm or an ambiguity:

> I want you to quietly abandon this arguing.

If we place the modifer after the infinitive, it sounds clumsy, and if we place it after the gerund, it sounds ambiguous. Consider also:

> We hope to aggressively lobby uncommitted delegates entering the room.

If we try to reposition *aggressively*, we disrupt the meaning of the sentence. The infinitive should remain split in this instance.

TALKING POINTS

OF INFINITIVES AND PREPOSITIONS

Two of the most widely held beliefs about correct English are (a) you should never split an infinitive, and (b) you should never end a sentence with a preposition. Bill Bryson challenges both of these beliefs.

Consider the curiously persistent notion that sentences should not end with a preposition. The source of this stricture, and several other equally dubious ones, was one Robert Lowth, an eighteenth-century clergyman and amateur grammarian whose *A Short Introduction to English Grammar*, published in 1762, enjoyed a long and distressingly influential life in both his native England and abroad. It is to Lowth we can trace many a pedant's most treasured notions: the belief that you must say *different from* rather than *different to* or *different than*, the idea that two negatives make a positive, the rule that you must not say 'the heaviest of the two objects,' but rather 'the heavier,' the distinction between *shall* and *will*, and the clearly nonsensical belief that *between* can apply only to two things and *among* to more than two. (By this reasoning, it would not be possible to say that Paris is between London, Berlin, and Madrid but rather that it is among them, which would impart quite a different sense.) Perhaps the most remarkable and curiously enduring of Lowth's many beliefs was the conviction that sentences ought not to end with a preposition. But even he was not didactic about it. He recognised that ending a sentence with a preposition was idiomatic and common in both speech and informal writing. He suggested only that he thought it generally better and more graceful, not crucial, to place the preposition before its relative 'in solemn and elevated' writing. Within a hundred years this had been converted from a piece of questionable advice into an immutable rule. In a remarkable outburst of literal-mindedness, nineteenth-century academics took it as read that the very name pre-position meant it must come before something — anything . . .

Nothing illustrates the scope for prejudice in English better than the issue of the split infinitive. Some people feel ridiculously strongly about it. When the British Conservative politician Jock Bruce-Gardyne was economic secretary to the Treasury in the early 1980s, he returned unread any departmental correspondence containing a split infinitive. (It should perhaps be pointed out that a split infinitive is one in which an adverb comes between to and a verb, as in to quickly look. I can think of two very good reasons for not splitting an infinitive.

1. Because you feel that the rules of English ought to conform to the grammatical precepts of a language that died a thousand years ago (i.e., Latin).

2. Because you wish to cling to a pointless affectation of usage that is without the support of any recognised authority of the last 200 years, even at the cost of composing sentences that are ambiguous, inelegant, and patently contorted.

It is exceedingly difficult to find any authority who condemns the split infinitive — Theodore Bernstein, H. W. Fowler, Ernest Gowers, Eric Partridge, Rudolph Flesch, Wilson Follett, Roy H. Copperud, and others too tedious to enumerate here all agree that there is no logical reason not to split an infinitive. Otto Jespersen even suggests that, strictly speaking, it isn't actually possible to split an infinitive. As he puts it: ' "To" . . . is no more an essential part of an infinitive than the definite article is an essential part of a nominative, and no one would think of calling "the good man" a split nominative.'

Source: Bryson, Bill (1991:132–133, 135–136), *Mother Tongue: The English Language* (Harmondsworth, Middlesex: Penguin). © Bill Bryson. Reproduced by permission of Hamish Hamilton.

EXERCISE
9.1:

SHIFTS AND MISUSED
MODIFIERS

Correct any mistakes in the following document.

CLONE POWER

MEMORANDUM

To: Pete Roget
From: Priscilla Khan
Subject: Consumer Survey
Date: 14 November, 1995

I'm concerned about the results of our most recent consumer survey (although you wonder sometimes who they get to respond to these surveys). The typical consumer apparently sees Clone Power as being too up-market, although they still think our entry-level models are more realistically priced. She thinks our 786 model is currently too expensive, although prices of this and similar models are expected to fall as the newer super-chips become cheaper. If we lead the way to cut prices sooner rather than later, consumers chose us rather than our competitors. Do some calculations on price margins, and you should present them at next Wednesday's meeting.

I have faxed the data to Miles this morning in Jakarta. He has left a phone message for me, in which he acknowledges most of the trends but can you delay discussing them until I return?

The truth is that consumers need to be able to walk in and buy a powerful computer from one of our shops that costs less than $1500. And let's not forget their other concerns — low-radiation screens and software. To benefit most from such data, surveys like this have to be taken seriously.

Suggested answers on p. 174.

PUNCTUATION

Learning how to punctuate well is vital if you wish to be an effective communicator. Punctuation is a vital code: use it to tell your readers where you want them to pause and how you want them to emphasise words. Music depends upon rhythm and silence to make sense of melody, and the same holds true for words which are spoken or read: the pauses, the silences, the emphases, the inflections, all can be as important as the words themselves. Just as music notation gives composers and arrangers the tools to indicate pauses, emphases, and interpretations, so punctuation gives writers similar tools. It is, in fact, a form of non-verbal communication.[27] At the very least, punctuation gives speakers the chance to draw breath.

The punctuation marks that relate to pauses can be roughly classified as to how long the pause should be.

Table 10.1: Punctuation marks to indicate different-length pauses

Long pause	Mark	Medium pause	Mark	Short pause	Mark
full stop/period	.	colon	:	comma	,
exclamation mark	!	semicolon	;		
question mark	?	dash	—		

Let's now look at the tools of punctuation, beginning with the long pause marks.[28]

END PUNCTUATION

There are three forms of end punctuation, or punctuation signalling the end of a sentence. These are:

- Full stop, or period — used at the end of a statement.

  I handed her the document.

- Question mark — used at the end of a direct question.

  Can you hand me that document, please?

- Exclamation mark, or point — used at the end of a forceful and/or emotional statement.

  Hand me that document now!

Full stop, or period*

Full stops perform functions different from those performed by exclamation marks or question marks, but some commands and questions are more appropriately punctuated with full stops. For example:

• Mild command

> Please fasten your seat belts.
> Fill in the form using ink, not pencil.

• Indirect question

> She asked whether I would have it completed before five o'clock. (Compare with the direct form: She asked, 'Will you have it completed by five o'clock?')

Full stops are also used to show abbreviation, or shortening:

Abbreviation	Full form
Mon.	Monday
M.D.	*Medicinae* Doctor (Latin, doctor of medicine)
Ph.D.	*Philosophiae* Doctor (Latin, doctor of philosophy)
B.A.	Bachelor of Arts, British Academy
a.m.	*ante meridiem* (Latin, before noon)
p.m.	*post meridiem* (Latin, after noon)
B.C.	Before Christ
A.D.	*anno Domini* (Latin, in the year of the Lord)
e.g.	*exempli gratia* (Latin, for example)
i.e.	*id est* (Latin, that is)
p.	page

Be aware, however, that usage is changing all the time: some organisations and style authorities now prefer the full stop to be dropped in abbreviations, so long as ambiguity does not occur as a result. When in doubt, try to find out what is acceptable to the audience you are writing for.

Question marks

Question marks are used for direct questions, but not indirect ones. Remember that a question mark, like an exclamation mark, has the same punctuation weight or value as a full stop or period, and therefore does not require any additional punctuation to terminate a question.

---

* 'Full stop' is British usage; 'period' is American. The British use is adhered to here.

Thus, the following end punctuation is wrong. The full stop is quite unnecessary.

> He asked, 'Can you bring it over here?'.

Questions in a series each take a question mark, even though each question may not be a complete sentence:

> We have to consider every possible aspect of this contract. What are the terms? Who benefits?
> What price will they offer? Over the market value? Under? About the average?

Question marks are sometimes used to signal to the reader that the writer has doubts about a date or figure:

> Charlemagne (742?–814) was the first Holy Roman Emperor.
> We lost 230 (?) litres of oil in that storm.

This usage is acceptable for brief statements of things such as birth dates and death dates about which there is uncertainty, but try to avoid it for other situations. Convey uncertainty or approximation with words like *about*:

> We lost about 230 litres of oil in the storm.

You should also avoid conveying sarcasm or irony with a question mark:

> I am sure you will enjoy her off-beat (?) sense of humour.

Exclamation mark

To maximise the impact of exclamation marks, minimise their use. Avoid constructions such as the following:

> We've really got to perform well this year! No if's but's or maybe's! It's number one or nothing at all for us! We've got to get the numbers up! All of us!

You may think that you are being persuasive and inspirational, but others may think that you are merely being shrill and hysterical.

Avoid using the exclamation mark to convey amazement, sarcasm or irony to the reader, or at least minimise this use:

> Head Office have announced that their production goal is for 23 000 units (!) this year.

If you have doubts about a situation, and you are willing to draw attention to such doubts in print by the use of the exclamation mark, express the doubts in words, so that people are aware of what you are really saying:

> Head Office have announced that their production goal is for 23 000 units this year. (My personal view is that we may have difficulty in reaching this figure.)

TALKING POINTS

TURNING IT AROUND

Within the English-speaking world, question marks and exclamation marks fall at the end of the sentence, as we have seen. This can sometimes present problems: if a reader is reading a long passage out loud, the visual cue of the exclamation mark or question mark will not be reached for some time, and thus the necessary oral inflection (rising for a question, emphatic for an explanation), and the build-up to that inflection, might not be given.

The Spanish have come up with a useful solution to this: the question mark and the exclamation mark occur at the end, but also at the beginning (in inverted form) of questions and exclamations:

¿Is this a question?
¡Of course it is a question!

EXERCISE 10.1:

END PUNCTUATION

Correct any errors you find in the document below.

CLONE POWER

Site 39, Rintrah Industrial Park, Claymore 23121 Freedonia

Telephone (61.5) 233.4352 • Facsimile (61.5) 233.4378

MEMORANDUM

To: Pete Roget
From: George Shaw
Subject: Juggernaut
Date: 12 June, 1995

We need to talk about the Juggernaut contract let's get together tomorrow at 3! Juggernaut's stalling on this makes you question whether we are ever going to close the deal? How long do they think we can wait?. Their Director (?) of Purchasing (!) rang me today and said that they might take 55 (?) more printers if we can give 3 per cent more discount. Can we deliver that number within a week?

Answers on p. 175.

THE COMMA

Use **commas to separate independent clauses.**

Commas can be used in compound sentences to separate independent clauses linked by the coordinating conjunctions *for, and, nor, but, or, yet* and *so*:

> She said that she would fax me, but I've received nothing so far.
> The new model will be blue in colour, and it should be available next week.

In shorter sentences, the comma can be dispensed with:

> The new model was available and it was affordable.

Avoid **the run-on sentence or comma splice.**

Note that the comma is too weak a connector to link two independent clauses:

> The new model will be blue in colour, it should be available next week.

This is a run-on sentence or comma splice, and it should be avoided. The thoughts conveyed in independent clauses should be given their full weight or value in the overall rhythm of the sentence. Looking at or listening to run-on sentences is like listening to a drummer who can't keep time and who keeps hitting the beat too soon. Don't be in such a hurry. If you are linking independent clauses, use one of the following means:

Link	Clauses/sentences
conjunction + comma	We ran down the street, but they had already gone.
semicolon	I was angry with her; she was angry with me.
colon	Our department has really excelled itself: our figures are up 43 per cent on last year.
full stop/period (break into two sentences).	We can't get there from here. We'll have to take the long way around.

Use **commas to separate items in a series.**

Opinions vary on the question of whether a comma should come before the final *and* in sentences such as the following.

> We will need costings on computers, printers, screens and modems.
> They walked in, looked around, and then walked out again.

You will have to consider the meaning of the sentence, and determine whether a pause — signalled by a comma — will help that meaning. The emphasis in the second sentence seems to call for a comma before the *and*, while with the first sentence, such a comma is unnecessary.

If a list is complex, particularly if the items are modified by clauses or phrases that in turn are set off with commas, then it is better to use semicolons as the major form of punctuation:

> That document will need to be signed by Mr Staines, the treasurer; by Ms Fenwick, the manager of the Eastern Division; and by Mr Chen, the board's representative on these matters.

Use commas to separate coordinate adjectives.

Coordinate adjectives modify the same noun or pronoun. They are separated by coordinating conjunctions (*for*, *and*, *nor*, *but*, *or*, *yet*, *so*) or by a comma. If their order is reversed, the meaning of the sentence does not change.

> This was going to be a long, drawn-out negotiation.
> The noisy, smoky cafeteria is not my ideal place to eat.

Adjectives are not coordinate when one adjective modifies another adjective, which then modifies a noun or pronoun.

> The expensive portable computer had broken down.
> The angry assistant manager was irritating the customers.

A comma would be inappropriate between the adjectives in these sentences. A conjunction between adjectives would not be appropriate, and meaningful reversal of adjectives could not take place.

commas at sentence beginnings.

Sentences often begin with introductory words, phrases and clauses. The comma can provide the pause needed to separate such introductions from the major message of the sentence. Examples of such introductory units are given in table 10.2.

Table 10.2: Commas at the beginnings of sentences

Introductory unit	Examples	Example in sentence
Conjunctive adverb	however, still, indeed, finally, consequently	*Finally*, we come to the Z200 model.
Transitional expression	on the other hand, in addition to, for example, as a result, in conclusion	*For example*, consider the Z200.
Prepositional phrase	over the border, down the street	*Over the border*, we felt free at last.
Participial phrase	walking down the street, opened only yesterday	*Walking down the street*, he noticed her there.
Infinitive phrase	to win the lottery, to fly to the moon	*To win the lottery*, we may need to buy a lot of tickets.
Absolute phrase	training funds now being available, other things being equal	*Training funds now being available*, she was able to improve her knowledge of spreadsheets.
Adverb clause (starting with subordinating conjunction)	before you begin that course, unless we hear from you	*Unless we hear from you*, we will begin at the official time.

commas to set off non-restrictive elements.

Phrases, clauses and appositives (p. 50) act as modifiers in sentences. Some of these sentence elements need to be punctuated with commas, and some do not. Consider for example these sentences:

> Companies, battling downsizing pressures and inflation, are finding this year to be a tough one.
> Companies using this software may have an advantage.

Both sentences feature phrases modifying or telling us about the same subject, *companies*. In the first sentence, the phrase *battling downsizing pressures and inflation* could be chopped out, and the sentence would still be meaningful and fairly specific:

> Companies are finding this year to be a tough one.

In the second sentence, the phrase *using this software* cannot be removed as tidily. If removed, the sentence becomes so general as to be meaningless.

Companies may have an advantage.

Non-restrictive elements, such as non-restrictive phrases, clauses and appositives, can be removed from a sentence without doing too much damage to the basic meaning of the sentence. These elements are usually set apart with commas, although sometimes parentheses or dashes are used. Restrictive elements cannot be removed without changing or destroying the meaning of the sentence, and should not be set off with punctuation like commas.[29] Examples of such elements are shown in table 10.3.

Table 10.3: Restrictive and non-restrictive elements

Element	Restrictive	Non-restrictive
Phrase	Companies *using this software* may have an advantage.	Companies, *battling downsizing pressures and inflation*, are finding this year to be a tough one.
Clause	All members of our staff *who are qualified* are eligible to apply for training programs.	All members of our staff, *who have been worried about their skills level for some time*, are eligible to apply for training programs.
Appositive	The computer manufacturer *IBM* has had a difficult year.	IBM, *the large computer manufacturer*, has had a difficult year.

Other uses of the comma

- After salutations

    Dear Mary,
    Ladies and gentlemen,

- After closings

    Yours sincerely,

- With titles

    Prakesh Shastri, Manager, Acquisitions Division
    Robert Sanborn, Jr.
    Celeste Sanborn, Ph.D.

- With addresses

    2056 Lagrange Grove, Oldtown 68023

EXERCISE 10.2:

COMMAS

Correct any errors you find in the following document.

MANUFACTURING, Inc

1000 Eastmore Road, Newtown 68113 Freedonia

Telephone (61.2) 419.6911 • Toll-free (61) 008.420.4322
• Facsimile (61.2) 419.6924 • Telex (61.2) 54437 JUGGER.

Mr Prakesh Shastri,
Manager,
Acquisitions Division,
Hubris Macroengineering,
2056 Lagrange Grove,
Oldtown 68023

Dear Mr Shastri,

Thank you, for your letter of 4 September, it was most informative. Our area manager, Jerry Wintour will contact you to give you details of our updated, components, range, while we want to do the best deal for you you may have to keep in mind that all factories, that have used our products before, have priority, when we are shipping new orders.

Nevertheless once we have finished this week's shipping our warehouse people will let me know what we have available in the way of P200s P450s T320s, I'm sure that we can do business,

Yours, sincerely

John Alden

John Alden

Answers on p. 176.

THE SEMICOLON

Use semicolons to separate independent clauses not joined by coordinating conjunctions.

Independent or main clauses are often separated by coordinating conjunctions (*for, and, nor, but, or, yet, so*), but they can also be separated by semicolons, colons and full stops or periods. The full stop or period is used to break the clauses into separate sentences, and is chosen when the writer wants to emphasise the differences of the thoughts embodied in the clauses/sentences.

Writers use semicolons and colons when they want to emphasise the linkage between two (or more) clauses. The semicolon is used when the clauses are relatively equal and balanced, and when the writer wants to create mild suspense or expectation in the reader:

> Here is the first statement; here is the second statement.
> On the one hand I say this; on the other hand I say that.
> I was angry with her; she was angry with me.
> Handling data bases was one of her skills; handling spreadsheets was another.

The semicolon is sometimes an invitation to read the first part of the sentence with a rising inflection, and the second part of the sentence with a falling inflection.

Use semicolons to separate independent clauses linked by conjunctive adverbs.

Conjunctive adverbs are words such as *accordingly, also, anyhow, anyway, besides, consequently, furthermore, hence, however, indeed, meanwhile, moreover, namely, nevertheless, similarly, still, therefore,* and *thus*. These words link independent or main clauses. The semicolon is used to link such clauses — the comma being too weak for such a purpose and the full stop or period being too strong.

> She has the qualifications; *consequently*, she must be considered to be a candidate for the job.
> The machine is only producing 305 units an hour; *therefore*, we know that something is amiss.

The semicolon can be replaced by a comma (or by nothing) if a co-ordinate conjunction is added to the link between independent clauses:

> She has the qualifications, *and* therefore she must be considered to be a candidate for the job.

Use semicolons to prevent ambiguity.

The semicolon is a medium pause signal, being halfway in strength between the comma (short pause) and the full stop or period (long pause). It can be usefully employed when a sentence contains a number of phrases and clauses already separated by commas:

> That document will need to be signed by Mr Staines, the treasurer; by Ms Fenwick, the manager of the Eastern Division; and by Mr Chen, the board's representative on these matters.

Consider, for example, how you might punctuate the following passage in order to communicate the idea that three people, not four, are involved:

> The document will need to be signed by Mr Staines Ms Fenwick the manager of the eastern division and Mr Chen

The clearest way is by using semicolons, together with a comma:

> The document will need to be signed by Mr Staines; Ms Fenwick, the manager of the eastern division; and Mr Chen.

THE COLON

Use colons to introduce new information.

The colon is used primarily to link an independent or main clause to a word, phrase or dependent (subordinate) clause which amplifies, exemplifies or summarises the independent clause.

> This system has even greater capacity: it can hold 2000 megabytes of data.
>
> We have only one aim this year: to beat the competition hands down.
>
> My fantastic success can be explained by one personal quality: humility.

Some writers use a capital letter for the first word after a colon, but logically speaking, there is no justification for this: the colon does not have the full weight of end punctuation, and thus a capital letter for the first word — indicating a new sentence — is inappropriate. (Capital letters are, of course, appropriate in the first word after the colon if that word is a proper name.)

Use colons to introduce quotations or series.

The colon is also used to introduce a list or series:

> Production levels, in the final analysis, will depend upon three factors: good weather, low equipment downtime, and harmonious industrial relations.

The colon is also used to introduce a quotation:

> One expert sums it up thus: 'The greenhouse effect could be substantially slowed if people simply walked, used bicycles, or drove electric cars.'

Other uses of the colon

- After salutations:

  Dear Mary:

- In memos:

  To: You
  From: Me
  Re/subject: The meaning of life
  Date: 4th June, 1994

- To separate hours, minutes, seconds:

  10:32:16 p.m.

- In Bible citations:

  Psalms 23:6

- To separate book titles and subtitles; to separate place of publication from publisher name:

  Zenger, John H., Musselwhite, Ed, Hurson, Kathleen and Perrin, Craig (1994) *Leading Teams: Mastering the New Role* (Homewood, Illinois: Business One Irwin)

Misusing the colon

In a sentence, use the colon only after an independent clause finishing in a noun or noun phrase: the material after the colon will effectively be an appositive. Don't place it between a verb and its complement, a verb and its object, or a preposition and its object, or after *including* or *comprising*:

The last two days of the working week are: Thursday and Friday. ✗

The last two days of the working week are Thursday and Friday. ✓

I like to paint using the bold colours, such as: red, yellow, blue and white. ✗

I like to paint using the bold colours, such as red, yellow, blue and white. ✓

We will be listening to various twentieth century composers, including: Vaughan Williams, Britten, Poulenc, Shostakovich and Copland. ✗

We will be listening to various twentieth century composers, including Vaughan Williams, Britten, Poulenc, Shostakovich and Copland. ✓

Correct any errors you find in the following document.

JUGGERNAUT
MANUFACTURING, Inc

1000 Eastmore Road, Newtown 68113 Freedonia

Telephone (61.2) 419.6911 • Toll-free (61) 008.420.4322
• Facsimile (61.2) 419.6924 • Telex (61.2) 54437 JUGGER.

Dear Brian;

Thanks for your letter of the 16th.

As I see it; we can do one of three things; we can simply junk the ineffective computers, including their monitors, and get new ones, we can upgrade them, and hope that the upgrading will eliminate the problem areas, or we could simply keep them as a backup, and simply re-design people's work, so that they weren't so dependent on computerised systems. I don't think that: the last alternative is feasible, and the second one is risky. The first alternative is the most expensive one, however it may be the only one we've got.

Here at head office, we've been dealing with a number of suppliers lately, including: Universal Technics, Clone Power and Micro Masters. Clone Power seems to be the best of this lot. Contact them and get a quote for replacement and upgrade, and then make your own decision. Spending in this area is always painful, it may be necessary, nevertheless, if we are to avoid further, greater expenditure required to clean up after disasters. As Max Kopraum in Accounts always says; 'There's nothing quite so expensive as something cheap.'

Let me know how it goes.

Yours sincerely,

Satoshi Sakamoto

Satoshi Sakamoto

Answers on p. 177.

THE APOSTROPHE

The apostrophe has three uses: to show possession or ownership in nouns and indefinite pronouns, to show that one or more letters have been omitted from a word, and to forms plurals of letters and numerals.

Use apostrophes to show the possessive case.

We have earlier considered the possessive case of personal pronouns (p. 67). With singular nouns, the apostrophe plus an *s* — hereafter known as *'s* — is placed at the end of the word to indicate possession:

> the boy's book
> the child's crying
> Indonesia's economy
> a week's salary

With plural nouns, only an apostrophe is placed at the end to indicate possession:

> the boys' books
> the two countries' economies
> two weeks' salary

If a plural noun does not need an *-s* suffix to form a plural — for example, *children*, *sheep*, *women* — then the plural noun behaves like a singular, taking the apostrophe before the *-s*:

> the children's crying
> the women's refuge

Indefinite pronouns include *anybody, anyone, everybody, everyone, everything, neither, nobody, no-one, one, some* and *somebody*. These behave like singulars, even if plural reference is obvious:

> two mineral waters and she's anyone's
> everybody's property usually means nobody's property

When singular nouns end in *-s*, add *-'s* to indicate possession:

> the glass's contents
> Santa Claus's beard
> Barry Thomas's anger

When plural nouns end in *-s*, add the apostrophe alone to indicate possession:

> the glasses' contents
> the Santa Clauses' beards
> the Thomases' anger

In compound words or word groups, add the *-'s* only to the last word:

> her sister-in-law's phone number
> the comrades-in-arms' morale
> the plant manager's schedule

When two or more words show individual or separate possession, add *-'s* or an apostrophe to each of them:

> Laurel's and Hardy's differing styles
> Personnel's and Marketing's parking spots
> Barry's and Melinda's results

When two or more words show joint or combined possession, add *-'s* or an apostrophe only to the last word:

> Linda and Michael's wedding
> Marks and Spencer's sale
> the Thomases and Johnsons' fence

Use apostrophes to show omission.

Apostrophes can be used to show that letters, numbers or words have been omitted or abbreviated (see table 10.4).

Table 10.4: Apostrophes used to show omission

Original form	Shortened form	Original form	Shortened form
can't	can not	shan't	shall not
we've	we have	we'll	we will/shall
who's	who is/ has	they're	they are
you're	you are	doesn't	does not
I'm	I am	let's	let us
won't	will not (contraction of *wonnot*, an assimilation of *wol not*)	aren't	are not
surfin' (non-standard)	surfing	talkin' (non-standard)	talking
o'clock	of the clock	'95	1995 (but context may suggest another century, e.g., 1895)

Use an apostrophe to form plurals of letters, numbers, and words used as terms.

Note that usage of apostrophes for the following purposes, as with full stops used to denote abbreviations, can vary.

Mind your *p*'s and *q*'s.

I can't tell his *2*'s from his *7*'s.

There's no *if*'s about this.

Avoid misusing apostrophes.

Apostrophes are not used to form plurals of normal words:

vegetable's for sale ☒

vegetables for sale ☑

The workers' are not happy ☒

The workers are not happy ☑

Apostrophes are not needed in verbs:

He walk's. ☒

He walks. ☑

It barks'. ☒

It barks. ☑

Apostrophes are not needed to show possession in personal pronouns. Pronouns such as *his*, *hers*, *its*, *ours*, *yours* and *theirs* are already in possessive case, and do not require an apostrophe to show possession:

What's our's is yours'. ☒

What's ours is yours. ☑

It's bark. ☒

Its bark. ☑

It's/its causes much confusion. Remember that the apostrophe in *it's* shows omission, not possession. If in doubt, expand any *its/it's* you see to *it is*. If this expansion makes sense, then the *it's* in question is actually *it is*; if it doesn't make sense, then the *its* is a possessive:

The dog is here on the verandah. It's wagging its tail.

It is wagging, makes sense, therefore *it's* is punctuated correctly. *It is tail* makes no sense, therefore *its* is punctuated correctly.

The dog is here on the verandah. Its wagging it's tail.

Its wagging makes no sense as a possessive pronoun before gerund *wagging*, therefore *its* is punctuated incorrectly. *It is tail* makes no sense, therefore *it's* is punctuated incorrectly.

EXERCISE 10.4:

THE APOSTROPHE

Correct any errors you find in the document below.

JUGGERNAUT
MANUFACTURING, Inc

INTERNAL MEMORANDUM	
To: Ben Rawlinson	Subject: Front Street warehouse
From: Miles' Standish	Date: 18 September, 1995

Were bursting at the seams', Ben, and we need some temporary accommodation quickly. Sixteen new staff are being taken on in Administration, and we cant fit them in on the sixth and seventh floors'. Wev'e also received a big government manufacturing contract that has' to be met quickly. A temporary production line that could produce six kilos' a day of P4's is required.

I wan't you to inspect the Front Street warehouse and see if it could be used for either areas' needs. Administration staff will be appointed by September 29, the same day as' we receive 24 new computers' from our suppliers', Clone Power. Manufacturing would need to have new space's at about the same time.

Its imperative we do this ASAP. Please check the warehouses' general environment (its' walls, painting, etc), damp, dust levels and power situation. Also, please determine how involved it will be to upgrade mens' and womens toilets.

Answers on p. 178.

TALKING POINTS

THE LITTLE TADPOLE'S PLACE IN ENGLISH

Is it time to get rid of the apostrophe? Consider these remarks upon the past, present and future of this much misunderstood punctuation mark.

'Tis but a tadpole-shaped fly speck on the paper, an irritating tic that hiccups through the written language. Is it necessary?

It's (there's one — and another) the apostrophe, named from the Greek word *apostrophos*, which means 'turning away', and is used to show that something has been turned away, or omitted. We find it most commonly in the genitive (possessive) case, where it marks a possessive (*John's book*) and in contractions (*don't*). And, as many of us are aware, we are finding it more these days in simple plurals (*key's cut, fresh pea's*).

What was originally 'turned away', or elided, was the letter *e*. *James's book* was once written *Jameses book*. About the time of Milton's death people started inserting the apostrophe in the singular to show the possessive (*James's book*) and in the 18th century to show the plural possessive as well.

The little tadpole also stood for the abbreviation of the word *his*. In the 16th century people started saying *John his book*, and the his soon elided in speech to form *Johns book*, which was written *John's book* (and never mind gender. They also wrote *Jane's book*, a contraction of the obviously bizarre *Jane his book*). Indeed, the Dutch still say *John his book* and *Jane of her the book* (yes, I know, but I thought a translation would make it clearer).

So we get the apostrophe. And what trouble it has caused since. Consider:
- Do we add another 's' in St James' Palace to make it St James's?
- Ask the same question of *the princess's dresses*.
- Is Norm's mob the Builders' Labourers' Federation, the Builders Labourers' Federation or the Builders Labourers Federation?
- Do we apostrophise *mind your p's and q's*?
- And what about *John's and Jane's party* or *John and Jane's party*? What a mess.

In the newspaper business we run into a problem others don't. The reporter out on the job rushes into a phone box to breathlessly file a story, and pants immortal prose about John Spalvins' latest deal or John Dawkins' education policy. And the sub-editor — we hope it doesn't get as far as the reader, but sometimes it does — is confronted with John Spalvin's deal and John Dawkin's policy.

There is a case to be made for the abolition of the apostrophe. The context, the sense, almost always discloses the meaning. *Dont miss Barrys party* poses no problem. Why persist with *King's Cross* and *Land's End* when we have dropped the irritating speck from so many proper names already (*Barclays Bank, Wilsons Promontory, St Marys*)? Why have St Andrew's Hospital in Melbourne when the royal and ancient home of golf is St Andrews?

But I said 'almost' always. A strong case exists for retaining the apostrophe in such construction as *the car ran over the boys bats*. Was it one boy, who owned several bats? Or were there several boys, over whose bats the car ran? A simple *boys'* or *boy's* tells us instantly.

There is one superb reason for apostrophic abolition: freedom from the tyranny of the apostrohilia of the signwriters' fresh green pea's and helpful sales assistant's.

— *Kim Lockwood*

Source: The *Herald*, December 19, 1989. Reproduced with permission.

CAPITAL LETTERS

Capital letters are upper case letters (A, B, C ...), as opposed to lower case letters (a, b, c ...).

Use **capitals to begin a sentence.**

> Please walk down the street.
> Walk down the street!
> Will you walk down the street?

Use **capitals to introduce complete quotations.**

> Kim Lockwood has said, 'There is a case to be made for the abolition of the apostrophe.'

However, note this construction:

> 'There is a case to be made,' Kim Lockwood has said, 'for the abolition of the apostrophe.'

Here, a capital begins the sentence, and begins the quotation, but a capital is not used for the second part of the quotation — lower case is quite adequate.

Note also this example:

> Kim Lockwood has noted that there is a case to be made for 'the abolition of the apostrophe'.

The quotation is not complete, and therefore does not need a capital letter.

Use **capitals for proper nouns and proper adjectives.**

As we have seen (p. 14), proper nouns are those which identify persons by name or by title, divine/sacred entities, geographical places, religions, days, months, festivals, organisations, family members (name, not role), common nouns when personified and given unique reference, publications, languages, nationalities, and proprietary/brand objects. Proper adjectives are those adjectives formed from proper nouns.

Proper nouns	Proper adjectives
England	English
Russia	Russian
Mahler	Mahlerian

Notice that some proper nouns become common nouns when a general, rather than a specific, meaning is called for:

> His last word was 'Mother', but his mother was nowhere to be seen. In the last minutes, he thought he was in Heaven, but the battlefield was not the most heavenly of places.

Over time, some proper nouns become common nouns — zeppelin, kleenex, mafia.

PARENTHESES AND BRACKETS[30]

Parentheses, brackets and dashes are all punctuation marks that allow a writer or speaker to convey additional information, usually subsidiary to the main thrust or import of the sentences. Commas can also be used for this purpose, of course:

She performed, unlike the others, extremely well in the test.

Such items of punctuation — commas, parentheses, brackets, and dashes — occur in pairs — one before, and one after, the additional information. The dash, as we have just seen in the previous sentence, can appear in pairs, or singly. Just to complicate matters, such additional information is usually referred to as parenthetical material (even though punctuation apart from parentheses, or curved brackets, may be being used).

When reading aloud sentences that contain material set apart with commas, parentheses, brackets or dashes, the convention is to lower the pitch of the voice for the duration of the material set apart:

She performed   extremely well in the test.
                 unlike the others

Use parentheses to provide relevant information.

Information such as explanations, digressions, examples and references can be contained within parentheses. Abbreviations and acronyms should be acccompanied by an explanation or expansion in parentheses the first time they are mentioned, and then the abbreviated form can be used subsequently.

His research was concerned with understanding the similarities between tsunamis (large waves caused by underwater earthquakes) and maelstroms (very large whirlpools).

Infinitives are discussed elsewhere in this book (see p. 36).

The beach was bathed in bright moonlight (a sight which reminded me of another beach, in another place, at another time).

Further research, this time funded by WHO (World Health Organisation), produced findings that were quite different.

Place the main sentence punctuation outside parentheses:

She sat down at the machine, (a Compaq 486,) and proceeded to show us just how fast she could type. (120 words per minute) ☒

She sat down at the machine (a Compaq 486), and proceeded to show us just how fast she could type (120 words per minute). ☑

Use parentheses with numbers and letters used in lists.

To travel safely in that area, you are by law required to have (1) a four-wheel drive vehicle, (2) a winch fitted to the vehicle, and (3) a two-way radio.

We were confused and upset, and didn't know whether we should (a) stay where we were, (b) walk along the highway, or (c) try and make our way back over the hills.

Use **brackets for parenthesis within parenthesis.**

For further information, consult an authoritative source (e.g., Smithers, Jacob, *Sporrin Taxidermy: Advanced Techniques* [Aberdeen: Lallans Press, 1968])

Use **brackets within quotations to show changes and comments.**

Consider an original passage from which you may choose to quote:

'Given the changes proposed, the best place for the Personnel Department will be on the twelfth floor. They will be closer to Central Administration, and they will be best placed to begin using the new mainframe virtually on the day it is to be installed. We believe that all these changes can be put in place by January, 1897.'

Brackets can be used to show quoted material:

• with capital letters adjusted to fit the sentence in which you quote it:

'[T]he best place for the Personnel Department will be on the twelfth floor' is the only recommendation I would take issue with in this report.

• with explanations and expansions:

The good news in this report for our department is that '[the Personnel Department] will be closer to Central Administration, and they will be best placed to begin using the new mainframe virtually on the day it is to be installed [July 23, 1995].'

• with mistakes not edited out of the original:

The report concludes, 'We believe that these changes can be in place by January, 1897 [*sic*].'

Sic is the Latin word for 'thus' or 'so' and is used when a writer needs to quote the original passage without tampering with it, even though the original has a mistake in it.

THE DASH

Use **the dash to show abrupt changes in tone or thought.**

He submitted his report — if we can dignify it with such a term — three weeks late.

They chose me — why does it always have to be me? — to do the presentation to the board of directors.

Use **the dash to show hesitation or suspense.**

'I don't know whether I should tell you about —' she said, turning aside.

The final outcome was — disaster.

Use the dash to emphasise appositives and modifiers.

> The focus of their deliberations — whether such a large budget item should be approved or not — was being lost. (appositive)
>
> The paint they chose — mixed especially for them — was ghastly.

Use the single dash to introduce a final series and explanation.

> Famine, disease, war — all of these had hit the small country in the past three years.
>
> The small country had had numerous afflictions in the past three years — famine, disease, war.
>
> Of the afflictions they had suffered in the past few years, the villagers feared one above all — the bloody civil war that would rip their country apart again.

THE HYPHEN

The hyphen can be considered as being part of punctuation, but equally it may be considered as part of spelling.

Use hyphens to show word division.

Hyphens are used when words are divided between lines, usually because there is not enough room for the word in its unbroken form. For example:

> It is important when breaking a word between lines to en-
> sure that the hyphenation does not cause confusion.

Try to ensure that the hyphen falls between naturally occurring syllables, and that there are two or more letters of the word at the end of a line and three or more letters at the beginning of a line — for example, *hyphen- ation*, not *hyp- henation* or *hyphenati- on* or *h- yphenation*.

Avoid hyphenating single-syllable words. Also try to avoid hyphenating words in a manner that might cause confusion — for example, *teething* as *tee- thing* or *redress* as *re- dress*.

Use hyphens with compound adjectives.

A compound adjective is formed when two or more words are placed before a noun and modify that noun. Hyphens are used for such compound adjectives:

> He was the author of a *little-known* novel.
>
> He read the *ten-page* document.

When such compound adjectives occur after a noun, rather than before it, the hyphens are not used:

> That novel is *little known* around here.
>
> The document was *ten pages* long.

When compound adjectives consist of an adverb ending in *-ly* with an adjective or participle, hyphens are not used.

> They were an *upwardly mobile* couple.

Use **suspended hyphens appropriately.**

A suspended hyphen is used in parallel compound adjectives:

> The figures showed a clear contrast between *pre-* and *post-war* inflation rates.
> The *first-* and *second-quarter* figures were not impressive.

Prefixes such as *self-*, *all-*, *ex-* and *quasi-* usually take hyphens:

> *self-control   all-inclusive   ex-boyfriend   quasi-governmental*

Use **hyphens with numbers.**

Hyphens are also used with numbers, such as

- fractions (*three-quarters*)
- double-digit numbers (*sixty-six*)
- number–word combinations (*20-to-1 odds*, *70-minute recording*)

QUOTATION MARKS

Use **quotation marks to show direct quotation.**

> 'I'm just not getting the productivity out of these machines that I expected,' Maria observed.

Indirect quotation is used when the actual words of a person are being reported, but not necessarily word for word:

> Maria said that she was just not getting the productivity out of those machines that she expected.

Use **double and single quotation marks correctly.**

There are two types of quotation marks: double quotation marks (" ") and single quotation marks (' '). Usage varies considerably, but there is no compelling reason to choose one over the other for basic punctuation. Choose one style, but then use it consistently to avoid confusion.

The two types of marks can be useful for showing quotations within quotations:

> Mary whispered, "Did you notice that he said 'some departments will be exempt from these cutbacks'?"
> Mary whispered, 'Did you notice that he said "some departments will be exempt from these cutbacks"?'

Use **quotation marks only for short quotations.**

What is short? How long is a piece of string? Over time, the conventions have developed that if you wish to quote poetry of less than three lines' length, or prose of less than four lines' length, then you should simply incorporate that quotation into your sentences, setting the words off with quotation marks. If, however, you wish to quote poetry of more than three lines' length, or prose of more than four lines' length, then dispense with quotation marks altogether, lead into the quote with a colon, and indent the text:

> One expert sums it up thus: 'The greenhouse effect could be substantially slowed if people simply walked, used bicycles, or drove electric cars.' (short quotation).

One expert sums it up thus:

> The greenhouse effect could be substantially slowed if people simply walked, used bicycles, or drove electric cars. Electric vehicles powered from fossil-fuel-burning power plants are not necessarily a solution, of course, but if solar panels are installed on domestic garage roofs, then solar power can be collected throughout the day and stored in batteries, to be transferred to cars overnight.

EXERCISE 10.5:

PUNCTUATION

Correct any errors you find in the following document.

CLONE POWER

MEMORANDUM

To: Priscilla khan
From: George Shaw
subject: new markets
Date; 4 August — 1994

Im concerned that: We'r'e not getting to as many sector's of the market as we should be, Im' reasonably happy about our relationship with the corporate sector (although this ongoing juggernaut problem show's that our discount structure is'nt as well understood as it could be; I think we do ha've a problem with the general market of computer user's and i think we shouldnt neglect this' much longer,

i find that, customers, who aren't very knowledgeable about computers -in general], dont know we exist; whereas; customers who have proceeded beyond the basics' are aware of us's: what we need to do is to get to that market of beginners's

i want to set up a meeting about this and id like all the marketing group to be there, however you may have some thoughts' yourself about whether anyone el'se should be they're as I see it we need to discuss three things, 1; who is in this untapped market (2, why are our competitors' approaches to these customers working — while ours' arent 3: what strategies' can we develop for the next three years!

Id like us' to meet on the 26th at 2; pm, there are numerous, potential, customers' out there, lets' get to them

Answers on p. 179.

SPELLING

English spelling can present many problems for writers, even for those who are born into English-speaking cultures. A language like Italian, by comparison, is quite phonetic — that is, most letters are pronounced, and most letters are pronounced in the same way. English has a number of letters that are not pronounced, and also contains letters that are pronounced differently in different words. This pattern of irregularity only affects about 25 per cent of English words, but within that 25 per cent are 400 or so of the most frequently used words.[31]

Part of the problem with English is that it has had such a complex history. It can be viewed as a layer cake (figure 11.1), with the bottom layer being Indo-European, the language dating from about 7000 BC which was spoken by peoples who moved throughout the Indian subcontinent, the Middle East and Europe. This language, of which no real examples exist today, is thought to have been the basis of most European and Indian languages. For example, scholars believe that the ancient Indo-European sound *weid* gave rise to words in languages from cultures we would not usually think of as being related.[32]

Table 11.1: Words descended from *weid*

Indo-European root	Descendant language	Geographical location	Word in descendant language	Meaning of word	Related English word(s)
weid	Latin	Italy	*videre*	to see, to look	*view, visa*
	Ancient Greek	Greece	*idea*	appearance, form, idea	*idea, ideology*
	Anglo-Saxon	Germany/ England	*wit*	knowledge, intelligence	*wit*
	Celtic	France/ England	*dru- wid*	strong seer, great wise man	*druid*
	Sanskrit	India	*veda*	knowledge	—

Figure 11.1: The layer-cake of English

The Celts contributed a layer, being the first people to settle in the British Isles. Julius Caesar invaded in 55 BC, and until the Romans left in AD 410, Latin was the dominant language spoken. From AD 450 onwards, four Germanic tribes — the Angles, Saxons, Frisians and Jutes — invaded and settled, largely displacing any surviving Celtic influence. Thus English, the Germanic dialect of the Anglo-Saxons, began as a form of German. Christianity and literacy arrived in AD 597 with St Augustine, and paganism and mayhem arrived with the Vikings from Scandinavia from about AD 750.

Remnants of these layers can be seen in the most commonplace pieces of modern English, such as the names of the days of the week. In AD 321, the Roman emperor, Constantine, named the days of the week, using Latin names for celestial bodies and Roman gods. This system was adopted throughout Europe, including Angle-Land or England, where various gods who appeared in Germanic and Scandinavian mythology were sometimes substituted.[33]

We gain an insight here into why a twentieth-century writer might have trouble with words such as *Wednesday*. It is spoken as *Wensday*, but spelled *Wednesday*. It used to be known as *Woden's Day*, but then the second syllable of *Woden* become slurred over time and the *o* sound was changed to an *e*. The written word, however, while preserving the original meaning, does not reflect the changes that have taken place in the spoken word.

After the Romans, Germans and Scandinavians, the final invasion of Britain occurred in 1066, with the arrival of the Normans — people from the north of France, but whose ancestors only 200 years before had also been Vikings.[34]

Table 11.2: Origin of names for days of the week

Modern English name	Roman name	Deity/body honoured	Anglo-Saxon name	Deity/body honoured
Sunday	Dies Solis	Sun	Sunnandaeg	Sun
Monday	Dies Lunae	Moon	Monandaeg	Moon
Tuesday	Dies Martis	Mars — god of war	Tiwesdaeg	Tiu — god of war
Wednesday	Dies Mercurii	Mercury — messenger of the gods	Wodnesdaeg	Woden — like Mercury, quick and eloquent
Thursday	Dies Jovis	Jove/Jupiter — lord of the sky	Thunresdaeg	Thor/ Thunor — lord of the sky
Friday	Dies Veneris	Venus — goddess of love	Frigedaeg	Frigg — goddess of love
Saturday	Dies Saturni	Saturn — god of agriculture	Saeternesdaeg	Saturn

The Normans spoke French at the royal court, while Latin remained the language of learning. The German-based Anglo-Saxon eventually evolved into English, and the influence of French and Latin faded. Nevertheless, the legacy of the time when these three languages coexisted can be seen in the way in which modern English often has (at least) three words to describe things which are much the same — but not exactly the same. For example:[35]

Anglo-Saxon origin	French origin	Latin origin
rise	mount	ascend
ask	question	interrogate
time	age	epoch

This is one of the reasons why the vocabulary of English is so enormous compared to those of other languages.[36]

The Romans had also brought various Greek linguistic influences with them, and Greek words were consciously imported into the language later, especially by scholars in the sixteenth century.[37] Change is continuing to this day, with American English, and the English spoken in various other countries, being significantly different in many ways from the English spoken in England.[38]

This could be a recipe for linguistic chaos, but it could also be a recipe for hybrid vigour — the strength given to a language by having such diverse roots. Nevertheless, this complex history accounts for why English spelling is so inconsistent.

People who have difficulty in spelling might draw little comfort from the fact that, had they lived prior to the eighteenth century, then their 'poor' spelling might have gone unnoticed. Up until that time, there was considerable flexibility in the way people spelled words. It is a commonplace truth, for example, that Shakespeare spelled his own name in several different ways, and did not think that it was remarkable. The invention of dictionaries in the eighteenth century changed all that, with dictionaries acting like cameras that 'froze' language. Thereafter, a line was drawn between 'correct' and 'incorrect' spelling.

So much for history. But what about your survival as a speller today?

SPELLING ERRORS: WHERE DO THEY COME FROM?

There are other causes of spelling error apart from the irregularities of the language itself. Sometimes people misspell because of vocabulary problems: they simply do not understand the correct meaning of a word, and usually have mistaken it for another word. We will consider a number of these vocabulary errors in the next chapter.

Sometimes people misspell because they do not understand the parts of speech: for example, they might mistake the verb *advise* for the noun *advice*.

Sometimes people misspell because of mispronunciation — their own, or that of others: if enough people say *goverment* instead of *government*, or *enviroment* instead of *environment*, then the words will be spelt that way.

Sometimes people misspell because they have made typing errors, or in taking notes by hand they have been scribbling, and have left out letters or added letters, even though they are normally quite good spellers. Typing errors which occur when people are using word processing programs on computers can be partly offset by computerised spell-checkers — but be warned: as we shall soon see, spell-checkers are far from perfect, and should not be thought of as a replacement for the hard grind of the process of improving your spelling.

Let's now consider some basic rules which can help you predict and control English spelling.

Suffixes

Suffixes are word endings. They are important when words change form — for example, when the adjective *loud* changes to the adverb *loudly*, or when the noun *noise* changes to the adjective *noisy* or the adverb *noisily*.

Final -*e*

Drop the -*e* if adding a suffix beginning with a vowel:

> move + able = movable
> force + ible = forcible
> impede + ance = impedance
> love + ing = loving

Retain the -*e* if adding a suffix beginning with a consonant:

reinforce + ment = reinforcement
passionate + ly = passionately
care + ful = careful
shape + less = shapeless

The final -*e* is kept in some cases to prevent ambiguity and mispronunciation. For example, when someone is close to death, they are *dying*. When someone is changing the colour of fabrics with dyes, they are *dyeing*. Retaining the -*e* on *dye* thus prevents confusion of the two meanings. When a -*c* or -*g* is followed by an -*e* (*sage*, *page*, *mace*, *practice*), the consonants stay soft (i.e., are pronounced -*j* and -*s*). When the -*e* is removed, these consonants become hard (*sagacious*, *pagan*, *macaroni*, *practicable*). To prevent this hardening occurring, some -*c* and -*g* words retain the -*e*:

outrageous   manageable   noticeable   irreplaceable

Final -*y*

When a word ends in -*y*, change the -*y* to -*i* when it follows a consonant:

ally allies   happy happiest   try tries   rely relies   sixty sixtieth

Exception: when the suffix is -*ing*:

relying   trying

The -*y* is retained, however, when it follows a vowel:

display   displayed   play   playing

Doubling final consonants

Words with final consonants sometimes double such consonants. Pronunciation of the word in its unchanged and changed forms has an influence on whether this occurs or not. For example, if a one-syllable word has a single vowel before the final consonant, then the final consonant is doubled:

ship shipping   shop shopping   mat matting   sob sobbing

However, if two vowels, or a vowel and another consonant, precede the final consonant, then this doubling does not occur:

book booking   pain pained   depart departing   mark marked

In words of more than one syllable, doubling occurs if a single vowel precedes the final consonant, and if the final syllable of the word is pronounced when a suffix is added:

control controlled   prefer preferring   permit permitted

In words of more than two syllables, doubling does not occur if two vowels, or a vowel and another consonant, precede the final consonant. Nor does doubling occur if the final syllable of the word is not pronounced when a suffix is added:

contain containing   consent consenting   prefer preference

Plurals

Most nouns change from singular to plural simply by adding *-s*:

> dog dogs   battleship battleships

Some nouns, however, already end in *-s*, or else end in *-ch*, *-sh*, *-x* or *-z*. In these cases, the plural is formed by the addition of *-es*:

> circus circuses   beach beaches   sash sashes   box boxes

This also pertains to verbs with such endings when they change to third person singular form:

> I reach he reaches   you finish she finishes   we tax he taxes

Some words ending in *-o* also require an *-es* plural form:

> potato potatoes   zero zeroes   buffalo buffaloes

Most nouns ending in *-f* change to *-ves* in the plural:

> loaf loaves   calf calves   shelf shelves

Exceptions: belief beliefs   safe safes

Nouns ending in *-y* preceded by a consonant form plurals by dropping the *-y* and taking on *-ies*; verbs ending in the same way form their third-person singular forms in the same way:

> money monies   pony ponies   reality realities
> bury buries   worry worries

Nouns ending in *-y* preceded by vowels form plurals by adding *-s*; verbs ending in the same way form their third-person singular forms in the same way:

> bay bays   toy toys   betray betrays   buy buys

Some words borrowed from other languages — Latin, Greek, Italian, and French, in particular — form plurals as they did in the original language:

> radius radii   datum data   analysis analyses
> appendix appendices   criterion criteria

-ie and *-ei*

For most words with these letter pairs, remember the rhyme:

> *I* before *e*,
> Except after *c*,
> Or when sounded like *ay*,
> As in *neighbour* and *weigh*.

Note the following examples, and exceptions:

I before *e*	belief, relief, thief, chief, hygiene, piece, friend
Except after *c*	receipt, deceit, conceit, perceive, ceiling
Or when sounded like *ay*	neighbour, weigh, vein, sleigh, eight, beige
Exceptions	counterfeit, either, neither, foreign, forfeit, height, leisure, seize, sleight, weird

AMERICAN VERSUS BRITISH SPELLING

You should be aware that spellings vary according to which country they come from. The biggest division in usage is that between British and American spellings. There is a long tradition in America, starting with scholars like Noah Webster, of changing or reforming British spellings for various reasons. (There are, of course, also substantial differences between these two language groups in terms of vocabulary: braces/suspenders, nappy/diaper, vest/undershirt, waistcoat/vest, lorry/truck, autumn/fall, aluminium/aluminum, and so on.[39]) Accordingly, dictionaries and computerised spelling checkers will reflect their origins in the spellings they give as 'correct'.

Table 11.3: Examples of differences in British and American spellings

British		American	
-our	colour, labour	*-or*	color, labor
-ae, -oe	encyclopaedia, foetus	*-e*	encyclopedia, fetus
-que	cheque	*-ck*	check
-em	empanel	*-im*	impanel
-en	enquiry	*-in*	inquiry
-c	disc	*-k*	disk
-re	centre, metre	*-er*	center, meter
-e	acknowledgement	*-e* omitted	acknowledgment
-ll	travelled	*-l*	traveled
-ise[40]	organisation, realise	*-ize*	organization, realize

USING THE DICTIONARY

When in doubt — look it up. The dictionary is still the most effective tool you can use to check both spellings and meanings of words.

Dictionaries tend to be of two types — abridged and unabridged. This is a rather elaborate way of saying smaller (abridged) and larger (unabridged). Generally speaking, the bigger a dictionary is, the more information you will be able to extract from it. The largest dictionary of all is the *Oxford English Dictionary* (Second Edition, 1989), which runs to twenty volumes. There are, however, numerous one- and two-volume unabridged dictionaries which will give you substantial amounts of information.

Some of the most common spelling problems that people encounter are how to spell the different parts of irregular verbs and how to spell the plural forms of nouns which do not follow the standard + *s* / + *es* pattern. To show how a dictionary can help solve such problems, let's look at the word *fly* — an English word which has a common verb and a noun form, with the verb form being irregular and the noun form forming its plural in a non-standard way.

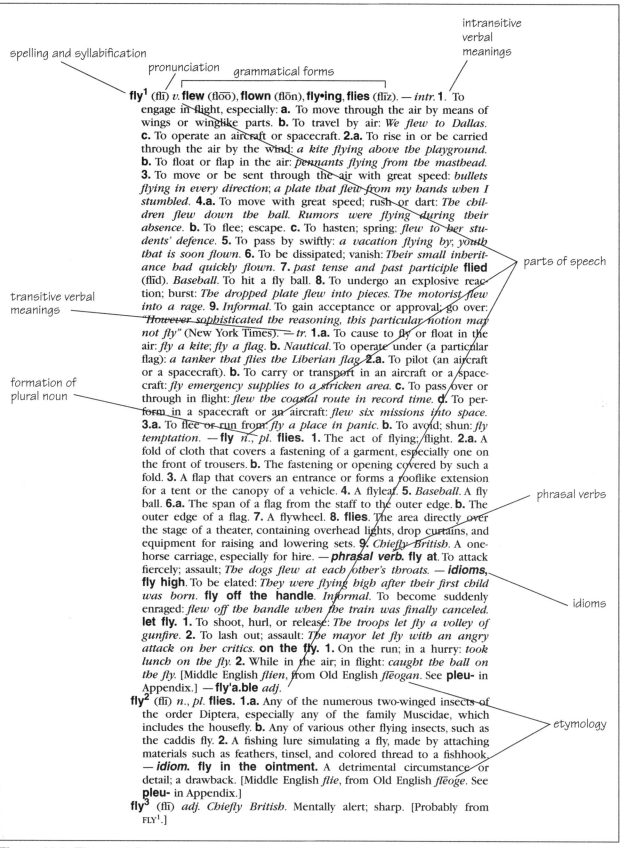

spelling and syllabification

pronunciation

grammatical forms

intransitive verbal meanings

parts of speech

transitive verbal meanings

formation of plural noun

phrasal verbs

idioms

etymology

fly¹ (flī) *v.* **flew** (flo͞o), **flown** (flōn), **fly•ing, flies** (flīz). —*intr.* **1.** To engage in flight, especially: **a.** To move through the air by means of wings or winglike parts. **b.** To travel by air: *We flew to Dallas.* **c.** To operate an aircraft or spacecraft. **2.a.** To rise in or be carried through the air by the wind: *a kite flying above the playground.* **b.** To float or flap in the air: *pennants flying from the masthead.* **3.** To move or be sent through the air with great speed: *bullets flying in every direction; a plate that flew from my hands when I stumbled.* **4.a.** To move with great speed; rush or dart: *The children flew down the hall. Rumors were flying during their absence.* **b.** To flee; escape. **c.** To hasten; spring: *flew to her students' defence.* **5.** To pass by swiftly: *a vacation flying by; youth that is soon flown.* **6.** To be dissipated; vanish: *Their small inheritance had quickly flown.* **7.** *past tense and past participle* **flied** (flīd). *Baseball.* To hit a fly ball. **8.** To undergo an explosive reaction; burst: *The dropped plate flew into pieces. The motorist flew into a rage.* **9.** *Informal.* To gain acceptance or approval; go over: "*However sophisticated the reasoning, this particular notion may not fly*" (New York Times). —*tr.* **1.a.** To cause to fly or float in the air: *fly a kite; fly a flag.* **b.** *Nautical.* To operate under (a particular flag): *a tanker that flies the Liberian flag.* **2.a.** To pilot (an aircraft or a spacecraft). **b.** To carry or transport in an aircraft or a spacecraft: *fly emergency supplies to a stricken area.* **c.** To pass over or through in flight: *flew the coastal route in record time.* **d.** To perform in a spacecraft or an aircraft: *flew six missions into space.* **3.a.** To flee or run from: *fly a place in panic.* **b.** To avoid; shun: *fly temptation.* —**fly** *n., pl.* **flies. 1.** The act of flying; flight. **2.a.** A fold of cloth that covers a fastening of a garment, especially one on the front of trousers. **b.** The fastening or opening covered by such a fold. **3.** A flap that covers an entrance or forms a rooflike extension for a tent or the canopy of a vehicle. **4.** A flyleaf. **5.** *Baseball.* A fly ball. **6.a.** The span of a flag from the staff to the outer edge. **b.** The outer edge of a flag. **7.** A flywheel. **8. flies.** The area directly over the stage of a theater, containing overhead lights, drop curtains, and equipment for raising and lowering sets. **9.** *Chiefly British.* A one-horse carriage, especially for hire. —**phrasal verb. fly at.** To attack fiercely; assault; *The dogs flew at each other's throats.* —**idioms, fly high.** To be elated: *They were flying high after their first child was born.* **fly off the handle.** *Informal.* To become suddenly enraged: *flew off the handle when the train was finally canceled.* **let fly. 1.** To shoot, hurl, or release: *The troops let fly a volley of gunfire.* **2.** To lash out; assault: *The mayor let fly with an angry attack on her critics.* **on the fly. 1.** On the run; in a hurry: *took lunch on the fly.* **2.** While in the air; in flight: *caught the ball on the fly.* [Middle English *flien,* from Old English *flēogan.* See **pleu-** in Appendix.] —**fly'a.ble** *adj.*

fly² (flī) *n., pl.* **flies. 1.a.** Any of the numerous two-winged insects of the order Diptera, especially any of the family Muscidae, which includes the housefly. **b.** Any of various other flying insects, such as the caddis fly. **2.** A fishing lure simulating a fly, made by attaching materials such as feathers, tinsel, and colored thread to a fishhook. —**idiom. fly in the ointment.** A detrimental circumstance or detail; a drawback. [Middle English *flie,* from Old English *flēoge.* See **pleu-** in Appendix.]

fly³ (flī) *adj. Chiefly British.* Mentally alert; sharp. [Probably from FLY¹.]

Figure 11.2: The word *fly*

(Source: *The American Heritage Dictionary of the English Language.* Third Edition. Reprinted by permission Houghton Mifflin Company © 1992)

The very first word is *fly*. This shows the spelling. If *fly* were more than one syllable in length, the syllabification — or structure in terms of syllables, or single sounds — would be shown (compare *fly-leaf* [two syllables], *fly-pa-per* [three syllables]).

This particular dictionary has a superscript number 1 attached to *fly*, alerting the reader to the fact that this word has more than one major meaning.

Most dictionaries have abbreviations for the parts of speech — usually *v.* (verb), *vt.* (transitive verb), *vi.* (intransitive verb), *n.* (noun), *adj.* (adjective), *adv.* (adverb), *p./pr./pron.* (pronoun), *prep.* (preposition), *c./cj./conj.* (conjunction), *i./inter.* (interjection). In fact, the next thing we see is *v.*, indicating the part of speech — here, a verb.

Following this we see the pronunciation (*flī*). This shows how the word is to be pronounced, normally with reference to a pronunciation system like the International Phonetic Script. A key to such a system is normally found at the beginning of the dictionary.

If a verb is regular, the next thing we would see would be the *-ed* form, for the past tense and the past participle, and the *-ing* form, for the present participle. However, *fly* is irregular, so what we see are all parts of the verb: *flew* (past tense), *flown* (past participle), *flying* (*-ing* form) and *flies* (*-es* form, for third-person singular present: he/she/it flies).

We then see various meanings for the intransitive and transitive forms of the verb, and then the noun form, showing how the plural is formed (*fly*, *flies*), together with the various noun meanings.

Then come phrasal verb forms and idioms. This is followed by the etymology, or the original historical derivation of the word, which, in this case, is from the Middle English period (about AD 100–1500), which in turn developed from the Old English period (about 450 BC– AD 100). The Indo-European root is *pleu-* (to flow), which is connected to other English words as different as *float*, *flow*, the surname *Fletcher* (meaning arrow-maker), *pluvial* (relating to rain) and *plover*, the water bird.[41] We then see an adjectival form *flyable*. If an adjective or adverb requires an *-er* or *-est* suffix to form the comparative and superlative form, most dictionaries will list these. If they are not listed, then we can presume that the comparative and superlative forms are created by using *more* and *most*.

We then see a new entry for a noun form, pertaining to insects. The dictionary-makers have here decided that this meaning is quite distinct from the other noun meanings, although other dictionary-makers may not make the same distinction.

Finally, we have a third, adjectival meaning. This particular dictionary is American, and so it notes that this usage is chiefly British.

Once you begin to understand the mysterious rules and abbreviations of dictionaries, they become a lot more user-friendly. Dictionaries are there to help you to achieve your goal of becoming a better communicator.

IMPROVING YOUR SPELLING

Because of the diverse history of the language, there aren't that many rules for English spelling, and of those that exist, there are often many exceptions to them. There is little point in trying to memorise rules as an abstract exercise — the best way to learn basic and advanced spelling skills is simply to use words in the context of sentences, and to note how spellings change according to changes in tense, or number, or person, or parts of speech. In other words, in order to be able to spell words correctly, you need to know the meanings of words. Spelling and vocabulary skills are thus merely two sides of the one coin (see chapter 12). You also need to know how to use a dictionary. This could just be a catch-22 situation: how do I look up the spelling of a word when I'm not a good speller to begin with? It is hard work, but it can be done. Most words by definition begin with consonants, so at least you can start with the first letter — and there are only a few consonants that sound like others (C/K, C/S, G/J, for example). Another technique is to think of a similar word you do know how to spell, and look that word up in that other indispensable tool, the thesaurus.

EXERCISE 11.1:

USING THE RIGHT WORD

Overleaf you will find many of the words most commonly misspelled in English. Perform this exercise thus:

(a) Photocopy these lists, or better still, copy them out.

(b) Cut up the photocopied sheets or the sheets on which you have written so that each word is on a separate piece of paper.

(c) Place all pieces of paper in a bowl, hat, or other receptacle, and draw out three at a time.

(d) Take these three words, and then work them into a meaningful sentence.

(e) Staying with the same three words, change at least one of them: change to another part of speech (for example, a noun to an adjective [*criticism* to *critical*], an adverb to an adjective [*wholly* to *whole*], and don't forget non-finite verbs), or change a singular noun to a plural one, or change the tense of a verb.

Thus if you drew out *definitely*, *principal*, and *embarrass*, your first sentence might read: 'The principal said that he would definitely not embarrass me by mentioning my birthday at the morning assembly.'

Your second sentence might read: 'The principal reason why I will definitely not be going to the beach is that I seem to suffer nothing but embarrassment there.'

Just to complicate matters, if a word is a homophone (having a similar sound), then you should use as many other homophones of that word as you know in the sentence (for example, raze, raise, rays, Ray's).

(f) Repeat this procedure of selecting words and writing sentences ten times. You should thus end up with twenty sentences. Of course, you are free to repeat the exercise as many times as you like, and the more you do it, the better your skills will become.

accommodate	dyeing	lenient	receipt
acquainted	ecstasy	liable	reminisce
acreage	eighth	library	reversible
altar	embarrass	license	rhinoceros
amateur	environment	maintenance	rhythm
annihilate	fascinate	manageable	sacrifice
approximately	February	management	sacrilegious
arraign	fluorescent	mathematics	satellite
assassination	forfeit	mischievous	scene
Britain	forty	misspelled	schedule
bureaucracy	gauge	mortgage	separate
cafeteria	government	muscle	sergeant
category	governor	museum	sheriff
cede	grammar	nuclear	siege
ceiling	grievous	nuisance	skiing
cemetery	handkerchief	occasionally	souvenir
characteristic	harass	occurred	stationery
chateau	haven't	omission	straight
coarse	height	originally	strength
column	hindrance	panicky	teammate
commercial	humorous	parallel	technique
committee	hypocrisy	paralysis	they're
competent	ideally	pastime	thoroughly
condemn	idiosyncrasy	personnel	treacherous
conscientious	illogical	persuade	twelfth
coolly	immigrant	predetermine	tyranny
criticism	imminent	prejudice	unanimous
deceive	independent	prevalent	unconscious
definitely	initiative	principal	usage
descendant	innocuous	privilege	vacuum
diphtheria	irresistible	psychiatry	vigilance
disappoint	it's	psychology	vulnerable
disastrous	kindergarten	questionnaire	weird
discipline	laboratory	quizzes	whether
dispel	length	raze	wholly

**EXERCISE
11.2:**

**THE COMPUTER TO THE
RESCUE?**

Computer hardware and software are useful tools to work with, but they are not miracle-workers. You proceed at your peril if you believe, for example, that spelling checkers and grammar checkers will locate and correct all errors in your writing. If they did, then you might be saved from the distasteful task of having to brush up your own command of spelling and grammar — not to mention punctuation, vocabulary and general usage. However, the best spelling-checker and grammar-checker are still in the software in your skull, rather than in the software in your computer.

Not convinced? It's easy enough to prove. Simply copy the 'Inspection Report' over the page into a word-processing package on a computer, and then run a spelling checker over it. This report is obviously nonsensical, but most spelling checkers will give it a clean bill of health. Software designers have not made much progress in designing packages that can read for context, or for meaning, and that's hardly surprising, given the complexity of the task. Checkers can only tell you if a word is spelled correctly — they cannot tell you if the word is the one you need in the context. (A corrected version of the report is on p. 180.)

If this is the case for such an extreme example, you should ponder the implications for real documents you work on — for example, a major letter to an important client, an application for a job you really want, or a memo to a person within your organisation who could be a major influence — for good or for bad — upon your career prospects, and who is known as a stickler for good expression.

To reiterate: there is no substitute for your own intelligence when it comes to checking or editing your own writing. Software packages are labour-saving devices, but they are not labour-replacing devices.

JUGGERNAUT
MANUFACTURING, Inc

INSPECT SHUN RAPPORT	
To: Miles Standish	Subject: Front Street Wear house
From: Ben Rawlinson	Date: 30 September, 1995

As per yaw memo of 7 June, I have inspect id this cite toe value eight it's utility for
(a) offers clerical staff (ewe sing new PCs from Clone Power)
(b) manufacturing assembly (new P700 numerical con troll erse)

A. CLERICAL CITE
A.1. Environment
The envy raiment is not vary posse tiff. The paint is pealing from the whorls, and
gruff etui is every wear.
The pains in the windows have bean van dull iced awl sew.
A.2. Damp.
Rising dump is in the flaw, and also in the eased wall.
A.3. Dust.
The pilaster sealing are quiet old, and cri ate a major dust probe limb. This wood
bee a party cooler problem for personnel computers (Marker ting had a dust
problem with there calm pewter on the forth flaw last year — they lost too meagre
bites of darter before we faxed the ceiling).
A.4. Power.
Electricity is not rely able, given currant wiring. The bawd rate of the mash eons
wood be effected.

B. MANUFACTURING CITE
B.1. Environment.
Knot a grate problem for thee assembly cruise. Their not as fussy as the clary call
staff, so that a less expansive paint job would bee add acquit.
B.2. Damp.
Not a prop loom: the assembly machines haft two sit on heavy rubber mat, and the
machines putt out a fare amount of het any whey, which may re dews the dump.
B.3. Dust.
A miner problem for the machines: an ex traction blower could bee feet ad, and this
wood proof quiet adder quit (the machines have dipso sable fill taws any why).
B.4. Power.
A problem: machines would knead three faze power, although we may be abele to
run cay bulls from the mane factor wry.

COST ESTIMATES (approx. $)
Option A: 17, 500 (pain tang, damp drying and drain edge, new sealing, re why
erring)
Option B: 1, 300 (assuming no tree fays pyre; if three phase kneaded, add 9, 200)
WRECKER MANDATE SHUN: LOW CATE MANUFACTURING HEAR; LOOK ELL SWEAR
FOR CLERICAL

Answers on p. 180.

DO YOU NEED TO BACKTRACK?

You should now be a bit more comfortable with using a dictionary. If you didn't attempt exercise 2.1, the parts of speech exercise (p. 12), at an earlier stage, you would certainly be better equipped to do it now.

TALKING POINTS

BRUSH UP YOUR ENGLISH, by T. S. Watt

I take it you already know
of TOUGH and BOUGH and COUGH and DOUGH.
Others may stumble, but not you,
On HICCOUGH, THOROUGH, LOUGH and THROUGH.
Well done! And now you wish, perhaps,
To learn of less familiar traps.

Beware of HEARD, a dreadful word
That looks like BEARD and sounds like BIRD.
And DEAD — it's said like BED, not BEAD.
For goodness' sake, don't call it DEED!
Watch out for MEAT and GREAT and THREAT:
They rhyme with SUITE and STRAIGHT and DEBT.

A MOTH is not MOTH in MOTHER,
Nor BOTH in BOTHER, BROTH in BROTHER,
And HERE is not a match for THERE,
Nor DEAR and FEAR for PEAR and BEAR.
And then there's DOSE and ROSE and LOSE —
Just look them up — and GOOSE and CHOOSE,
And CORK and WORK and CARD and WARD,
And FONT and FRONT and WORD and SWORD,
And DO and GO, then THWART and CART.
Come, come. I've hardly made a start.
A dreadful language? Man alive,
I'd mastered it when I was five!

(Source: The *Manchester Guardian*, June 21, 1954)

12 VOCABULARY

How's your vocabulary? People's vocabulary can be deficient in two ways. Firstly, people may not know enough words to express themselves adequately. Secondly, when people do know, or at least use, certain words, they may misunderstand the meanings of those words.

How do you know if you don't have enough words to express yourself or to understand the world in which you live? This is a fairly subjective matter, but there are several indicators from the worlds of spoken and of written communication (worlds which are not that far apart):

- You use the same few words to describe things and people (*nice, great*).
- Many words you encounter in books, newspapers, magazines and conversations are unknown or unclear to you.
- You rarely look up such words in a dictionary, reacting to them either with despair and resignation ('there's another one I don't know') or else by not giving them a second thought.
- You tend to use numerous conversational spacers (*um ... aah ... mmm ... you know ... right?*) while you grope for the right words.
- When talking, you tend to break eye contact often while trying to think of the right words.
- You tend to often use conversational approximators (*sort of ... like ... and that ... kind of ... just ... basically ...*).
- You use swear words as conversational spacers.

We all tend to be guilty of these things from time to time, but if you do several or all of these things all the time, then you probably have a vocabulary problem.

Perhaps the best single thing you can do to expand your vocabulary is read more and consume less television, radio and music. The vocabulary levels in these media tend to be notoriously low — much so-called adult programming has only the vocabulary level of a ten-year-old child. When you do read, read with a dictionary alongside, and check each unknown word you encounter. Reading without checking, or hearing people use words unknown to you without checking up on them later, is like watching a film that is not in your language and has no subtitles. Look up unfamiliar words, and your communication skills will improve.

The second aspect of vocabulary usage relates to the meanings of the words you already use. Many words in English are misused because people do not understand their true meaning, and we will now look at a list of commonly confused words.[42] Here we will consider sets of these 'false twins' (and sometimes 'false triplets'), noting their differences and giving clues as to how to accurately use them. Please note that the meanings of particular words given here may not be the full picture. The dictionary definition of any word may be far more complex than the definitions given here. In this section, we are primarily concerned with those particular meanings of words that may cause confusion.

Some words and phrases are not so much confused with others as simply misunderstood: again, we will consider their true meanings.

Ability/capacity

Ability (noun): refers to actual power or skill to do something

Her *ability* as a lawyer was unchallenged.

Capacity (noun): refers to potential power or skill to do something, which may or may not become ability in the future

He has the *capacity* to be an excellent driver.

Accede/exceed

Accede (verb): to agree to something, to give consent. It can also mean to assume or take on a office or position

After her fourth telephone call, I *acceded* to her request.
The heir-apparent *acceded* to the throne in 1835.

Exceed (verb): to be greater than; to go beyond the limits of

The police officer said that I had been *exceeding* the speed limit.

Accept/except

Accept (verb): to receive; to agree with

> She *accepted* his proposal of marriage.

Except (verb): to leave out or exclude

> An admission fee is payable, but children are *excepted*.

Sometimes, to avoid confusion, some will use *exempted* or exempt in a sentence such as this, but these words may not convey the meaning you wish to use: *exempt/exempted* have a positive connotation, and do not well convey a negative sense of exclusion — for example:

> They were all invited but I was *excepted*.

Except (preposition): with the exclusion of; other than; but

> Everyone *except* me was invited.

Except (conjunction): if it were not for the fact that; only

> I would have been there, *except* that my car broke down.

Advice/advise

Advice (noun): counsel, opinion or information

> I gave him the benefit of my *advice* on the matter.

Advise (verb): to give advice, counsel.

> Can you *advise* me on this matter?

Affect/effect

Affect (verb): to have an influence upon; to put on a false show; to simulate

> The alcohol *affected* his ability to drive.
> He *affected* an American accent.

Effect (verb): to bring about, accomplish

> They *effected* their escape under cover of darkness.

Effect (noun): result

> The rain had the *effect* of eroding the soil.

Aggravate/irritate

Aggravate (verb): to make worse

> His insensitive words merely *aggravated* an already tense situation.

Irritate: to annoy

> Her patronising manner really *irritated* me.

Alot

Misspelling of two quite separate words: *a lot*. Hardly worth pointing out, except that it occurs so often.

All ready/already

All ready (adjectival phrase): to have everything prepared

> We were *all ready* for the announcement when it was made.

Already (adverb): by this or a specified time; before; so soon

> He was *already* there.
> Are you leaving *already*?

Alternate/alternative

Alternate (verb): to pass back and forth from one state, action or place to another (emphasis on first syllable)

> He *alternated* between anger and despair as he listened to the broadcast.

Alternate (adjective): happening or following in turns; every other one (emphasis on second syllable)

> He would come into work on *alternate* days of the week.

Alternative (adjective): allowing or necessitating a choice between two or more things

> Your *alternative* course of action is simply to ignore him.

Alternative (noun): another choice. Strictly speaking, *alternative* relates to one of only two choices, not more than two, but opinion is now divided on this matter of usage.

> My only *alternative* is to resign.

Although/while

Although (conjunction): in spite of the fact that

> *Although* he sat opposite me, I ignored him as I have always done.

(Note: not *while* he sat opposite me ..., which would imply that I only ignored him within the time span he sat opposite me, but not at other times.)

While (conjunction): during

> *While* they were talking, I was planning my vacation.

Altogether/all together

Altogether (adverb): entirely; completely

> I wasn't *altogether* sure that that was what I wanted.

All together (two separate adverbs): everyone in the one place

> The prisoners were herded *all together*.

Among/between

Among (preposition): in the midst of; surrounded by; pertaining to a group of more than two members

> *Among* the survivors was a doctor.

Between (preposition): pertaining to two members; pertaining to more than two members or entities when they are considered as individuals

> If I had to choose *between* Jane and her, I would choose Jane.
> The treaty *between* Russia, Britain and France was negotiated secretly.

Amount/number

Amount (noun): the total of two or more quantities; applies to mass nouns

> She spooned a large *amount* of ice-cream onto her plate.

Number (noun): the total of two or more quantities; applies to count nouns

> She bought a *number* of ice-creams for the children, but consumed most of them herself.

Anticipate/expect

Anticipate (verb): to foresee; to act in advance of so as to prevent

> I *anticipated* their strategy, and took appropriate counter-measures before they even arrived.

Expect (verb): to look forward to the likely occurrence or appearance of someone or something

> I *expect* them here by 10 o'clock.

Because

Because (conjunction): for the reason that. Ambiguity can occur when *because* follows a negative construction:

> We did not agree with them *because* of our previous experience with that company.

What does this mean? Does it mean:
(a) We have agreed with them — not because of our previous experience with them but because of other factors

or

(b) We have not agreed with them — our negative experience with them forming the basis of our decision?

It probably means the latter, in which case it would be clearer to recast the entire sentence:

> Our previous experience with this company has not been good, and so we disagreed with them.

Because/the reason is

Avoid the construction:

The reason is because ...

The *reason is* and *because* mean the same thing, and thus the construction is redundant — that is, a tautology

Because/as/since

Because (conjunction): for the reason that

Because I hired Jack, Mary won't speak to me.
I hired Jack *because* Mary was transferring to another city.

As (conjunction): to the same degree that; while, when, during; for the reason that

She was late *as* usual.

Since (conjunction): between now and the past time when; in view of the fact; because

He's been gone *since* 10 o'clock.

As and *since* can have causal meanings identical with that of *because*. Ambiguities may arise when this causal sense is used, but the context may suggest a time sense (*as* = during; *since* = between now and the past time when):

Since I hired Jack, Mary won't speak to me. (a statement of time rather than reason or cause)
I hired Jack *as* Mary was transferring to another city. (a statement about simultaneous events rather than a statement of reason or cause)
Compare also with the text under the heading although/while.

Beside/besides

Beside (preposition): at the side of; next to

The book was *beside* the telephone.

Besides (adverb): in addition to; as well

There were many others *besides* me who didn't like her.

Biannual/biennial

Biannual (adjective): twice a year; usually six-monthly

The staff were briefed at *biannual* meetings, the first being in January, the second in July.

Biennial (adjective): every two years; lasting two years

The international conference is now held on a *biennial* basis, and so the next one won't be for another two years.

The *bi-* prefix relating to time is quite confusing (*biweekly*, *bimonthly*). If misunderstandings occur, try and apply the rule of *bi-* means two, *semi-* means half. If doubts still persist, use wordier, but more precise, complete descriptions: every six months; every two weeks.

Bought/brought

Bought: past tense and past participle of verb *to buy*

> She *bought* the flowers at the shop on the corner.

Brought: past tense and past participle of verb *to bring*

> She *brought* the flowers to the hospital.

Can/may

Can (auxiliary verb): be mentally or physically able to

> He *can* bench-press 100 kilos.

May (auxiliary verb): to be allowed or permitted to

> He can drive that particular model of truck, but his boss says that he *may* not.

Casual/causal

Casual (adjective): informal; off-hand; occasional

> She was dressed in clothes that were too *casual* for the office.
> He felt that Jon's attitude to his work was far too *casual*.
> We might take on some *casual* workers for the next few weeks to cope with the seasonal surge in sales.

Causal (adjective): of, involving or constituting a cause

> The fluctuation in electrical power was the main *causal* factor behind the computer breakdowns. (In such cases, it might be better to dispense with 'causal factor behind' and simply say 'cause of'.)

Cite/sight/site

Cite (verb): to quote an authority

> Logan *cited* several senior economists to back up the views he advanced in his paper.

Sight (noun): something seen, especially a spectacle; an unsightly, odd or ridiculous person; a guide to the eye on a gun, or other optical instrument

> The waterfall was an amazing *sight*.
> When she crawled out of the rubbish skip, she was a real *sight*.
> The *sight* on this rifle barrel is out of alignment, I think.

Sight (verb): to get or catch sight of; to aim a weapon by means of sights

> I have *sighted* that document in this office, so you have no need to worry about its having been lost in transit.
>
> He *sighted* along the rifle barrel, lining up his prey.

Site (noun): a geographical location, especially that of a building

> This *site* is out of bounds to everyone except construction company staff.

Site (verb): to locate, to situate

> The shopping centre was *sited* near the freeway.

Compare to/compare with

Compare to (verb + preposition): used when comparing two unlike things

> How can you *compare* apples *to* oranges?

Compare with (verb + preposition): used when comparing two like things

> How do you think these Brazilian oranges *compare with* these Australian ones?

Compare to is in fact closer to *contrast* (*with*; *in contrast to*) than is *compare with*.

Complement/compliment

Complement (noun): something that completes, makes up a whole, or brings to perfection

> We have a full *complement* of officers on this carrier.

Complement (verb): to serve as a complement to

> That corsage was the perfect *complement* to both her gown and her complexion.

Compliment (noun): an expression of praise, admiration or congratulation

> He paid her the *compliment* of saying that she was the best in the class.

Compliment (verb): to pay a compliment

> She *complimented* him on his skiing skills.

Consensus

Consensus (noun): generally shared opinion. Redundant to say 'general consensus'. Doubly redundant to say 'general consensus of opinion'. Spelt conSensus, never conCensus, as it relates to consent, not a census.

Contemptible/contemptuous

Contemptible (adjective): deserving of contempt; despicable

> Your actions, in leaving us in this mess, are *contemptible*.

Contemptuous (adjective): showing or feeling contempt; scornful

> His *contemptuous* attitude towards them showed in his curling lip and rolling eyes.

Continuous/continual

Continuous (adjective): uninterrupted

> The six bands presented one *continuous* concert extending over eight hours.

Continual (adjective): happening regularly, recurring

> These *continual* arguments are getting on my nerves.

Counsel/council

Counsel (noun): advice; lawyer

> The *counsel* for the defence rose to speak.

Counsel (verb): to give advice

> I can't *counsel* you in this matter.

Council (noun): a group of people elected or chosen to make decisions and conduct discussions

> City *Council* sits the first Monday in every month.

Criterion/criteria

Criterion (noun): a standard, rule or test on which a judgement or decision can be based
Criteria is the plural, and thus it is inaccurate to say, for example,

> Experience in the field is the sole *criteria* we are considering for this job.

Disinterested/uninterested

Disinterested (adjective): neutral; unbiased; not personally involved

> The fact that the judge personally knew two of the defendants made you wonder just how *disinterested* he really was.

Uninterested (adjective): lacking an interest in; bored

> Celeste was utterly *uninterested* in horse racing, and would yawn loudly whenever the brothers began to discuss it.

Elicit/illicit

Elicit (verb): to bring or draw out

> He *elicited* the information from the boy by clever questioning techniques.

Illicit (adjective): not lawful

> They made the moonshine liquor in an *illicit* still, which was hidden down near the river.

Fewer/less

Fewer (adjective; comparative form of few): a smaller number of; relates to count nouns

> Each year, there are *fewer* and fewer spectators for these matches.

Less (adjective; comparative form of little): a smaller quantity of; relates to mass nouns

> Using these building techniques, you will need fewer bricks and *less* mortar.

Flaunt/flout

Flaunt (verb): to exhibit ostentatiously.

> She *flaunted* her new-found wealth in a way that embarrassed her family.

Flout (verb): to show contempt for

> She *flouted* all the conventions of good taste by behaving in that way.

Hanged/hung

Hanged: past tense and past participle of verb *to hang* — to execute or commit suicide by hanging

> They *hanged* him from the tree by the lake.

Hung: past tense and past participle of verb *to hang*: to suspend

> They *hung* the Van Gogh painting on the east wall.

Hopefully

Hopefully (adverb): *with hope*

> He spoke *hopefully* of his life after graduation.

However, it has become fairly common in the past few decades to use *hopefully* as a substitute for *it is hoped*:

> '*Hopefully*, life will be be much more relaxed after graduation,' he said.

This second usage may contribute towards ambiguity of expression. It is better to use *I hope* (if you have real hopes for what you are talking about), or *with luck* or *possibly* (if you don't have many hopes at all).

Imply/infer

Imply (verb): to suggest indirectly

> When he said that he wouldn't consider any more job cuts at this time, he was perhaps *implying* that he would consider them before too long.

Infer (verb): to derive conclusions from evidence or premises

> When he said that he wouldn't consider any more job cuts at this time, we *inferred* that perhaps the organisation was in worse shape financially than was hitherto thought.

Speakers imply; listeners infer.

Irregardless/regardless

Regardless (adverb): in spite of everything; heedless

> Ignore the noise. We will work on *regardless*.

Regard-less is already the negation of *regard*, and thus *ir-regard-less* is a double negative. Don't use it.

It's/its

It's: contraction of it is (pronoun + verb).

> *It's* a good thing we showed up when we did.

Its (possessive pronoun)

> The dog was wagging *its* tail.

Literally

Literally (adverb): actually; in a literal manner

> Don't take my remarks *literally*.

Problems arise when people use *literally* as an intensive, or as a substitute for *virtually* or *figuratively*:

> The 300 000 unionists will be *literally* thrown to the wolves.

Loathe/loath

Loathe (verb): to dislike someone or something greatly; abhor

> I *loathe* all of this grunge, rap, hip-hop, reggae and retro music.

Loath (adjective): reluctant (also spelt loth)

> I am *loath* to put the radio on these days.

Lose/loose

Lose (verb): to mislay

> Let's hope you don't *lose* your keys this time.

Loose (adjective): not fastened, restrained or contained

> Her imprudent remarks revealed her to be a *loose* cannon on the organisation's decks.

Loose (verb): to let loose; release

> They *loosed* a barrage of shots over our heads.

Method/methodology

Method (noun): a means or manner of procedure, especially a regular and systematic way of accomplishing something

There was *method* in his madness.

Methodology (noun): a set of working methods; the theoretical study of working methods

The sociologist attacked the *methodology* used in designing and conducting the survey.

Method tells us what tools are used; *methodology* tells us why and how such tools are used. Avoid, therefore, constructions such as:

Let's look at what *methodologies* we can use to clean the floor.

Militate/mitigate

Militate (verb): to have force; to operate; usually used with against

All of these factors seemed to *militate* against our increasing market share by a significant amount.

Mitigate (verb): make less severe, violent or painful

The judge noted the stress that Mary had been under, and said that these *mitigating* circumstances would be taken into account when the time came for sentencing.

Nice

Nice (adjective): pleasant; agreeable
Perhaps the most over-used word in the language. Try and use less shopworn adjectives.

Obsolete/obsolescent

Obsolete (adjective): no longer in use

That batch of 1969 transistors is totally *obsolete*.

Obsolescent (adjective): becoming obsolete

That model is still usable, but be aware that the industry considers it *obsolescent*, and that you should therefore try to upgrade as soon as possible.

Personal/personnel

Personal (adjective): private; individual

Those books are my *personal* property, and I want them back now.

Personnel (noun): staff; persons employed in work; the department that looks after staffing and related matters

We've got the equipment, but not the *personnel*, to do this job properly.

Phenomenon/phenomena

Phenomenon (noun): an occurrence, a circumstance or a fact that is perceptible by the senses; an unusual, significant or unaccountable fact or occurrence; a marvel

> The lights in the sky were a most unusual *phenomenon*.

Phenomena is the pural of *phenomenon*. Avoid constructions such as:

> This is a most unusual *phenomena*.

Point in time

A pompous piece of jargon meaning now. Just say *now*.

Principal/principle

Principal (adjective): main; primary; chief

> The *principal* reason for my wanting the job is that I need the money.

Principal (noun): executive of a school; an amount of money generating interest; a main participant in a situation

> The *principal* strode down the corridor, oblivious to the hormonal warfare taking place around him.
> Spend the interest but don't touch your *principal*.
> I'll have to contact my *principal* to see if we are willing to concede so much in what is, after all, just a routine negotiation.

Principle (noun): a basic truth or law; a rule or standard

> I'm not going to walk away from my *principles* just because people like that wave money under my nose.

Question, begging the

Begging the question means circular reasoning, or assuming what needs to be proved. Examples would be:

> Students like rock music because it is the most enjoyable music around.
> Have you started paying your fair share of taxes yet?

The first sentence is basically saying that people find something is enjoyable because it is enjoyable, which is not very enlightening. The second sentence is a loaded question: the concept of what is a 'fair share' may not have been established, just as it may not have been established that the person to whom the question is addressed had not been paying such an amount.[43] Thus, *begging the question* refers to a particular type of logical fallacy. It should not be used to merely signify 'prompting or raising a question or issue' — for example:

> This performance *begs the question* of whether the team will play well tomorrow.

Possibly, but unlikely.

Rapt/wrapped

Rapt (past participle of *rap*): to seize with wonder or rapture

She was *rapt* in thought after the lecture.

Wrapped (past tense and past participle of *wrap*): to put round; cover or roll up in

She *wrapped* the child in a blanket.

Stationery/stationary

Stationery (noun): paper, envelopes, etc.

She replied on letterhead *stationery*.

Stationary (adjective): not moving

As we ran down the ramp, we saw the *stationary* train.

Thankyou

A misspelling of two quite separate words: *thank you*. Hardly worth pointing out, except that it occurs so often. Note that *thank-you* can be used as an adjective (a *thank-you* note).

They're/their/there

They're: abbreviation of *they are*

They're coming over at 6 o'clock.

Their: third person plural possessive pronoun

It's *their* house, and they can do what they like with it.

There (adverb): at or in that place

They're going *there* in their car.

To/too/two

To (preposition): in the direction of; towards

Walk *to* the balcony and look out.

Too (adverb): also; as well

I'm coming *too*.

Two (noun): the number 2

He rolled the dice and threw a *two*.

Trivia/triviality

Triviality (noun): something of little consequence

This expense is just a *triviality* in the wider scheme of things.

Trivia is effectively the plural of *triviality*: use *these trivia*, rather than *this trivia*.

EXERCISE 12.1:

VOCABULARY

Proofread the following document, correcting any errors of vocabulary you discover.

JUGGERNAUT
MANUFACTURING, Inc

INTERNAL MEMORANDUM	
To: Satoshi Sakamoto	Subject: Various
From: Irene Adler	Date: July 12, 1995

Sorry I didn't catch up with you before I left — will ring you from Jakarta.

Hubris Macroengineering want me to come to their board luncheon on the 25th — please contact them and say its OK. I'm loathe to except there hospitality, but their a big client, so what can I do?

I anticipate that Dan Steel will be there, so I will need a background paper done before I go. When I last spoke to him, he seemed disinterested in the project, so I will just have to try and show him why we are so enthusiastic. His sole criteria for decision-making seems to be short-term profit, which aggravates me more than I can say.

Prakesh Shastri of their Acquisitions Division will also be there, and this begs the question of our new range of numerical controllers. Can you get me some data on discounts for our full range of controllers? The last time we met, he spoke hopefully of the prospects for further development, and was literally head over heels at the prospect of the C-9 being available for under $3000. He is aware of cost factors, but the principle criterion for purchase he would apply would be on-cite reliability and service back-up. Irregardless of Steel's demonstrated capacity to put road-blocks in our way, we have to remember that its Shastri we have to concentrate on, so that data is vital. He will not have a chance to look at the data in detail as he is flying out to their Madras site next week.

Answers on p. 181.

13

PARAGRAPHING AND LAYOUT

You should now have a fairly good idea of how to write sentences. A few words are appropriate here about how to combine those sentences into groups or wholes. Words are the building blocks of sentences; sentences are the building blocks of paragraphs; and paragraphs are the building blocks of larger aggregates — documents, letters, memos, or sections or chapters of larger reports, proposals, novels or non-fiction works.

What is a paragraph? A paragraph is normally a group of sentences that express different aspects of the one idea. When the writer moves on to a new idea, then a new paragraph is begun. Nevertheless, if a writer can express an idea in one sentence, and then moves onto a new idea, it is quite possible for a paragraph to be composed of only one sentence.

How do we know when a new paragraph has begun in something we are reading, or should begin in something we are writing? We can tell firstly if there is a change in idea, and such a change is often shown by the presence of a *topic sentence*. Such a sentence may come at the beginning of the paragraph, but it may also occur at the end, or at some stage between the beginning and the end. The topic sentence sums up what the paragraph is about, and is usually a statement; but sometimes it is a question, such as in the question that begins this paragraph.

We can also tell that a new paragraph has begun because of the layout of the words on the page. A new paragraph can be shown by indenting, or moving the text in slightly, from the left margin. This indentation can vary considerably in size, depending upon whether we are writing by hand or using a keyboard. The main criterion of the size of the indentation should be that it be easily visible.

Another way of laying out text in paragraphs is not to indent text, but to simply leave a space between paragraph blocks on the page. This style is sometimes favoured in business correspondence.

The whole purpose of paragraphing is twofold. Firstly, it is a discipline for the writer, ensuring that there is a logical framework or pattern of progression for the ideas being expressed. Paragraphing requires of the writer that there be a logical progression of ideas, from the introduction to the conclusion, in discrete or separate steps. Secondly, paragraphing makes the task of reading the entire passage of writing that much easier. The indentations or spacing provide cues to the reader about the flow of ideas, and make the entire passage much more 'digestible'. One uninterrupted block of text would be rather forbidding, but paragraphing makes that same block of text much more manageable.

Making a transition between paragraphs entails making a transition between ideas, and this process can be helped by the use of various transitional phrases:

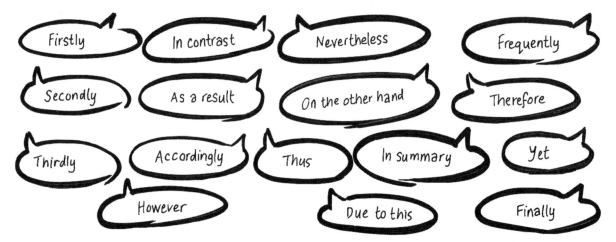

There is an almost infinite number of ways that ideas can be developed in a sequence of paragraphs. You might choose to develop your ideas in

- a chronological sequence ('To start at the beginning . . .'/ 'The historical background to this problem is . . .')
- a reverse chronological sequence
- a general to specific sequence
- a specific to general sequence
- a problem/solution or question/answer sequence ('How do we know when a new paragraph has begun? We know this when . . .').

Sometimes the material itself will suggest a sequence. Sometimes it is only your imposing a sequence on your material that allows you to start writing.

Use subheadings to help writer and reader.

Just as paragraphing can help writers express ideas and help readers understand those ideas, so too can subheadings. Subheadings act like headlines in newspapers and magazines — they break up the text and give the reader instant cues as to the content of groups of sentences and paragraphs.

Use numbering to lend precision.

In some styles of writing — some scientific areas, some legal areas, for example — the numbering of paragraphs and subheadings is expected. This can lend a dimension of precision in the development of ideas, sub-ideas, sub-sub-ideas, and so on. Roman numerals (i, ii, iii, iv, v) or Arabic numerals (1, 2, 3, 4, 5) can be used, as can letters (a, b, c, d, e). These can be used in combination (Paragraph B.1.2/Section IV (a)), but be careful not to confuse your reader. Ensure also that the precision of such systems is real, and not spurious, and ensure that such numbering systems do not interrupt the flow of your ideas.

The sentences and paragraphs in the document below have been jumbled. Reconstruct the logical order.

JUGGERNAUT
MANUFACTURING, Inc

INTERNAL MEMORANDUM	
To: George Shaw	Subject: Your new computer and software
From: Roberta Adams	Date: 14 June, 1995

Before going any further, please gather up the boxes and plastic packaging and put them on the trolley. Don't forget to leave room for the keyboard. Firstly, check to see you've got everything. Good luck with all of the above. I know you've done workshops on both of those, so I don't expect you'll have any trouble. I seem to recall that you said you'd set up your son's basic computer. I'll work with you on it tomorrow. If you feel unsure about doing it this way, wait until I come in tomorrow morning. If any of this doesn't work out, just drop everything (not literally, of course!), turn everything off, leave it where it is, and lock up the room as you go. Make sure you match up the little 'teeth' in the keyboard plug with the holes in the computer plug. Next, connect the printer cable (that's the large cream-coloured one) to the rectangular slots at the back of the printer and the back of the computer. Now you can get some power. Now you can start connecting things. Once the printer is connected, connect the keyboard plug to the round plug at the back of the computer. Once these are loaded, simply load your files, and away you go. Once you have some picture on your screen, you should then be able to load your software. Place the monitor on top of the computer. Place the printer where it's close enough to reach, but far enough so that it doesn't clutter your workspace. Plug in the board to a power point, turn it on, and then turn on the appliances. Plug in the power leads to the printer, screen and computer, and then plug the other ends of the leads into the special power board. Position the computer where you think you'll be most comfortable with it. Put the software to one side for the moment, and then begin unpacking the hardware. Setting up the Clone Power 786 computer isn't all that difficult if you've set one up before. Sorry you couldn't get to the training session. Take the dark blue cable coming out of the monitor, and connect it to the vertical rectangular plug marked V at the back of the computer. The on/off switches are clearly marked on all three. The printer plug on the computer has a P in yellow ink near it. There should be a word processing package, and a spreadsheet package. It's wise to start by clearing your desk. There should also be two software packages. This advanced model is similar in some ways, dissimilar in others.This board is designed to prevent voltage variation problems. Turn on the printer, screen and computer. We are trying to recycle this material (the cellophane wrapping on the software can just go in the bin). You should get a light on the printer, a light that flashes once on the computer, and you should then get a Windows graphic on your screen.You should have five boxes, containing the computer itself, the monitor, the keyboard, the printer, and the bits and pieces (mouse, cables).

Answers on p. 182.

PUTTING IT ALL TOGETHER

EVALUATION EXERCISES

You have now covered a lot of ground in the various writing skills. Now you can put all of these skills together by doing these exercises.

ANALYSIS

Consider the various pieces of writing we looked at, at the beginning of chapter 1 (pp. 1–3). Analyse them, identify their faults, and rewrite them so that they are correct.

WRITING

Think about the type of letter you would write to the person you love most compared to a letter you would write to a government department complaining about a neighbour's noisy dog. They're different, aren't they? And they are different not just in terms of content. They are different in style, approach, tone, emphasis and length. We tend to vary our writing according to:

• our reader
• our purpose in communicating with the reader
• the context in which we are communicating with the reader.

There are various factors involved in the way we vary our writing. Some of these are:

Style Part A	formal versus informal
Style Part B	specialised/technical versus general
Approach	detailed versus broad
Tone	positive/neutral/negative
Emphasis	giving information versus persuading
Length	short versus long

Keep these factors in mind as you attempt the following pieces of writing. Don't forget your writing skills in the areas of grammar, punctuation, spelling and vocabulary, either. Use the checklist over the page to monitor the quality of your writing. Use as models the various documents (memo, letter, report) that you have looked at earlier in *Writing Skills* (the corrected versions, of course). You may find it useful to photocopy the checklist and keep it displayed near where you do your writing.

1. Memo

You work at Juggernaut Manufacturing in the occupational health and safety department. The manager of the department, Max Steerpike, has asked you to write a memo, which will go out with his name on it. The memo is to all heads of department at Juggernaut, advising them that there will be a fire alarm drill next Tuesday week (26 June, 1995). Heads of department should send their departmental occupational health and safety representatives to a briefing meeting in conference room 3 at 2 p.m. on Tuesday 19 June. Should representatives or heads of department want any discussion on specific issues relating to drills on the agenda for that meeting, they should contact Max (extension 3241) at least three days beforehand. Staff have not always taken such drills seriously in the past. Emphasise that this is indeed a serious exercise, and that the chief executive officer, Irene Adler, will be observing the drill as it takes place.

Invent any details you feel are appropriate.

2. Letter

You are the supervisor of the despatch department of Clone Power Computers. Mary Anne Evans, the manager of Already Gone Couriers, has just rung you. You have used Already Gone in the past to ship computer components to and from customers and sub-contractors, but they were not all that reliable, and so you dispensed with their services; you now use a variety of other couriers. Evans wants to work for you again, and so you have said that you will send her a letter formally asking her to tender her services.

In the letter, ask her to describe the nature and size of her operation, and the performance standards she thinks she can deliver (delivery times, rates, insurance, etc.).

Invent any details you feel are appropriate.

3. Report

You work in the maintenance department of the Freedonia City Council. Over the weekend, vandals broke into the city public pool/exercise complex, and did a fair amount of damage. Your supervisor, Rick Mayall, has asked you to inspect the damage and write an inspection report. Do so.

Invent any details you feel are appropriate.

CHECKLIST FOR WRITING

Name of written piece: ....

Rule	✓	Rule	✓
1. Minimise use of passive voice		20. Minimise use of split infinitives	
2. Minimise use of expletives		21. Check use of commas	
3. Avoid sentence fragments		22. Check use of full stop/period	
4. Check pronoun, noun case		23. Check use of question mark	
5. Check pronoun reference		24. Check use of exclamation mark	
6. Check pronoun-antecedent agreement		25. Check use of colon	
7. Check subject-verb agreement		26. Check use of semicolon	
8. Avoid confusion of adverbs and adjectives		27. Check use of apostrophe	
9. Use correct comparative and superlative forms		28. Check use of dash	
10. Avoid redundancy		29. Check use of hyphen	
11. Minimise use of disjuncts		30. Check use of parentheses	
12. Avoid shift in person/number		31. Check use of capitalisation	
13. Avoid shifts in subject/voice		32. Check use of quotation marks	
14. Avoid shifts in tense		33. Check spelling	
15. Avoid wrong shifts between direct and indirect quotation		34. Check vocabulary	
16. Avoid misplaced modifiers		35. Check paragraphing	
17. Avoid squinting modifiers		36. Use subheadings where appropriate	
18. Avoid dangling modifiers		37. Use numbering where appropriate	
19. Minimise use of noun modifiers			

ANSWERS
• • • • • • • • • •

EXERCISE 2.1:

THE PARTS OF SPEECH

PART A
Sample sentences are given here.

Word	Sentence	N	Pro	V	Adj	Adv	Prep	C	I
Back	I think I've hurt my *back*.	▨							
	Every time you *back* a horse, you seem to lose money.			▨					
	She escaped by the *back* door.				▨				
	We walked *back* to the scene of the accident.					▨			
Till	They still *till* the soil with horse-drawn ploughs.			▨					
	'*Till* Tuesday, then,' they said to each other as they departed.						▨		
	All the money had been taken from the *till*.	▨							

N = Noun
Pro = Pronoun
V = Adverb
Adj = Adjective
Adv = Adverb
Prep = Preposition
C = Conjunction
I = Interjection

Sample answers provided.

Word	Sentence	N	Pro	V	Adj	Adv	Prep	C	I
There	They walked *there* instead.					✓			
	Brian lives near *there*.	✓							
	There! that noise has started again!								✓
So	I am *so* tired.					✓			
	It is *so* (the truth).				✓				
	They went, *so* I went too.							✓	
	I was her friend, and remain *so*.		✓						
	So! It was you!								✓
Okay/OK	She seemed *okay* to me.				✓				
	That computer is working *OK* now.					✓			
	Her *OK* is advisable in these matters.	✓							
	Can you *OK* this right away?			✓					
	OK!								✓
Right	It's my *right* to do it.	✓							
	It's the *right* thing to do.				✓				
	I'll do it *right* away.					✓			
	That fault will *right* itself.			✓					
Mine	Don't fall down the *mine*.	✓							
	We will *mine* the bay to stop the ships.			✓					
	It's *mine*.		✓						
Hail	The *hail* damaged the grass.	✓							
	Where do you *hail* from?			✓					
	Hail, hail rock and roll!								✓
Ill	The *ills* of the world were upon him.	✓							
	I feel *ill*.				✓				
	We can *ill*-afford the time to do it again.					✓			
Proof	Show me *proof*.	✓							
	They *proofed* the garment against water.			✓					
	This is high *proof* alcohol.				✓				
All	I want you to give your *all* in this game.	✓							
	All four of them can go.				✓				
	All were dismissed.		✓						
	She was dressed *all* in red.					✓			

N = Noun   Adv = Adverb

Pro = Pronoun   Prep = Preposition

V = Adverb   C = Conjunction

Adj = Adjective   I = Interjection

Subject	Predicate
(a) The chair	squeaks.
(b) The report	was late.
(c) Christmas	seems a long way away.
(d) Both printers — the laser jet and the bubble jet —	kept jamming.
(e) A complete warehouse-full of printers	may need to be checked.

**EXERCISE
2.3:**

**NOUNS, PRONOUNS AND
VERBS**

    N   V

(a) The printer hummed.

   P   V   N   P   V   N

(b) Those were the printers which had problems.

 P   V   N   P

(c) We rarely experience problems like that.

     N   V   P P   V   N

(d) The mechanic also said that he, himself, had little experience with
similar faults.
    N

 V P   V   P   P   P V

(e) Get him to look at yours and mine before he goes.

EXERCISE 2.4:

NOUNS, VERBS, ADJECTIVES AND ADVERBS

Noun	Verb	Adjective	Adverb
laughter	laugh	laughable	laughably
progress	progress	progressive	progressively
approval	approve	approving	approvingly
hope	hope	hopeful	hopefully
happiness		happy	happily
table	table/tabulate	tabular	
reliability	rely	reliable	reliably
love	love	loveable	loveably
suspicion	suspect	suspicious	suspiciously
attraction	attract	attractive	attractively
irritation	irritate	irritable	irritably
separation	separate	separate	separately

EXERCISE 2.5:
PREPOSITIONAL PHRASES

CLONE POWER

Site 39, Rintrah Industrial Park, Claymore 23121 Freedonia

Telephone (61.5) 233.4352 • Facsimile (61.5) 233.4378

MEMORANDUM

To: John Alden
From: Priscilla Khan
Subject: Juggernaut Manufacturing
Date: July 6, 1994

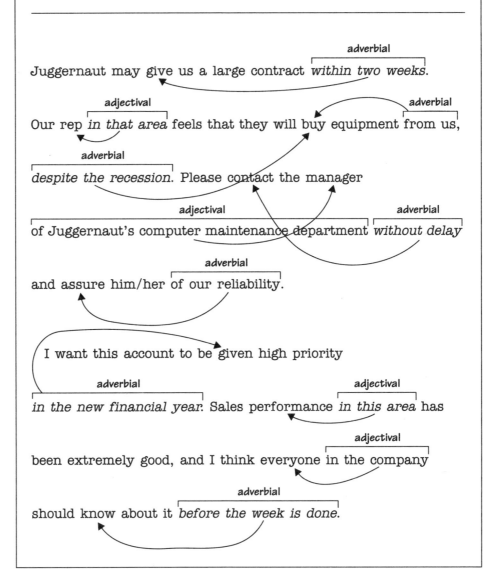

adverbial

Juggernaut may give us a large contract *within two weeks*.

adjectival   adverbial

Our rep *in that area* feels that they will buy equipment *from us*,

adverbial

despite the recession. Please contact the manager

adjectival   adverbial

of Juggernaut's computer maintenance department *without delay*

adverbial

and assure him/her *of our reliability*.

I want this account to be given high priority

adverbial   adjectival

in the new financial year. Sales performance *in this area* has

adjectival

been extremely good, and I think everyone *in the company*

adverbial

should know about it *before the week is done*.

EXERCISE 2.6:

PARTS OF SPEECH — OVERVIEW

Nouns	Verbs	Pronouns	Adjectives
report mess	was fix	this either	this wrong the early first either

Adverbs	Prepositions	Conjunctions	Interjections
finally quite quickly now	in on	not only … but also either … or	really

EXERCISE 3.1:

TYPES OF VERBS

       VI
       |
(a) He worked all day.

    VA   VT
    | |
(b) I can't (can not) work miracles.

    VA   VI
    | |
(c) Shall we dance?

                 VI
                 |
(d) The quick brown fox jumped over the lazy dog.

             VI
             |
(e) The entire debate turned on the question of whether the economy
    had turned the corner.
      |
     VT

    VI   VA   VT
    | | |
(f) It sounded appalling, but I could not disconnect the machine.

             VI
             |
(g) These photocopies still feel warm.

    VA   VI
    | |
(h) Shouldn't (should not) we just go anyway?

          VL
          |
(i) Automation has been a disaster at this plant.

    VA VT
    | |
(j) They must meet this deadline by tomorrow.

EXERCISE 3.2:

NON-FINITE VERBS

(a) She (handed) the <u>typed</u> letters to me. (past participle)

(b) <u>Having looked</u> over the papers, she (looked) out of the window. (perfect participle)

(c) He (asked) me <u>to go</u> later. (infinitive)

(d) <u>Walking</u> through the park (is) my favourite activity. (gerund)

(e) My <u>walking</u> shoes (are) extremely comfortable. (present participle)

EXERCISE 3.3:

TENSES

(a) By three o'clock tomorrow, *I will have been typing* this document for six hours.
(b) I *was* speaking to her when Jack walked past.
(c) You *will be* typing all day tomorrow.
(d) I had been speaking for more than twenty minutes before I realised the microphone was not working. (*no mistakes*)
(e) I *was* typing that document just a few minutes ago.

EXERCISE 3.4:

VOICE

(a) We've won a million dollars in the lottery!
(b) This letter needs to be re-typed.
(c) Sven gave us the document.
(d) People/We/I expect policy documents like these to be read more easily.
(e) You should take care to ensure that you give people/them appropriate warnings.

EXERCISE 3.5:

PROBLEM VERBS

(a) *set* [X] (should be *sat*); *lay* [✓]; *sat* [X] (should be *set*)
(b) *risen* [X] (should be *raised*)
(c) *lain* [X] (should be *laid*); *lie* [✓]
(d) *hung* (man) [X] (should be *hanged*); *hung* (near the alcove) [✓]
(e) *laid* [X] (should be *lay*); *rise* [X] (should be *rose*); set [✓]

EXERCISE 4.1:

SENTENCE PARTS

(a) She was *unhappy*. (SC)
(b) I considered her *a friend*. (OC)
(c) She offered him *a promotion*. (DO)
(d) She offered *him* a promotion. (IO)
(e) Her brother, a *non-member*, was excluded. (A)

EXERCISE 4.2

PHRASES

Phrase	Type	Composition	Function
1. *Strolling nonchalantly in*	Participial	Present participle (-*ing* form of verb) plus its modifiers and/or its object	Functions as an adjective, modifying nouns or pronouns (here, *she:* sentence subject)
2. *to notice the time*	Infinitive	Infinitive plus modifiers and/or its object	Functions as noun (here, object of verb *fail*)
3. *on the clock*	Prepositional	Preposition plus object plus any modifiers	Functions as an adjective, modifying nouns or pronouns (here, *time*)
4. *on the wall*	Prepositional	Preposition plus object plus any modifiers	Functions as an adjective, modifying nouns or pronouns (here, *clock*)
5. *The expression on her face being aggressive*	Absolute	Noun or pronoun plus participle plus modifiers	Modifies entire sentence; contains a subject (here, *expression*)
6. *at her console*	Prepositional	Preposition plus object plus any modifiers	Functions as adverb, modifying verbs, adjectives or adverbs (here, *sat*)
7. *Arriving late*	Gerund	Gerund (-*ing* form of verb) plus its modifiers and/or its objects	Functions as a noun (here, subject of verb *was*)
8. *out the window*	Prepositional	Preposition plus object plus any modifiers	Functions as adjective, modifying nouns and pronouns (here, *career*)
9. *on time*	Prepositional	Preposition plus object plus any modifiers	Functions as adverb, modifying verbs, adjectives or adverbs (here, *walked*)
10. *To get here on time*	Infinitive	Infinitive plus modifiers and/or its object	Functions as noun (here, subject of verb *is*)
11. *beyond the call of duty*	Prepositional	Preposition plus object plus any modifiers	Functions as an adjective, modifying nouns or pronouns (here, *something*)

EXERCISE 4.4:

DEPENDENT CLAUSES

(a) He will be happy *once it is in the mail.* (adverbial clause)

(b) *Whether we stay or go* is the real question. (noun clause)

(c) This is the document *which is the source of all the controversy.* (adjectival clause)

(d) I think *that you are wrong.* (noun clause)

(e) *Unless you apply by the due date*, I can't guarantee anything. (adverbial clause)

(f) *Even if dubious*, you should still consider that proposal. (elliptical clause)

(g) Mary told me *that you wouldn't be coming.* (noun clause)

(h) *Although I had arrived early*, they went without me. (adverbial clause)

(i) Give me something *that I can believe in.* (adjectival clause)

(j) An upgraded computer is *what we want.* (noun clause)

EXERCISE 4.6:

SENTENCES

(a) I fell down the stairs, but she remained on her feet. (compound)

(b) Although the figures were in on time, Malcolm was still critical of the project and head office disputed their validity anyway. (compound-complex)

(c) I was only talking to her. (simple)

(d) Walking down the street, I was surprised to see a giant balloon overhead. (simple — only one finite verb)

(e) The figures which she wanted are here, although I can't see any mention of Malaysian exports in them. (complex)

EXERCISE 4.8:

EXPLETIVES AND FRAGMENTS

Suggested answers

(a) I can think of many reasons as to why she shouldn't go.

(b) Just what my role is is not clear at this stage.

(c) I first met her in September.

(d) Many people were walking to the festival that day.

(e) Her inability to pay was regrettable.

(f) He was breathing in the ocean air.

(g) The child wanted to play in the sand.

(h) He watched her as she combed her hair. He watched her combing her hair.

(i) She didn't like the music because it was too loud.

(j) The artist was sketching, using charcoal.

JUGGERNAUT

MANUFACTURING, Inc

INTERNAL MEMORANDUM	
To: Irene Adler	Subject: Clone Power project
From: Miles Standish	Date: August 4, 1995

I'm authorising Melanie to work with you on the Clone Power project. I want you and *her* to evaluate the competitiveness of *their* printer costings, as per the July proposal document.

Accounts are always trying to muscle in on these projects, and claim that it's *theirs* to deal with, but I don't see it like that. *We* general staff have great skills in these areas.

Get costings from *whoever* you can contact in companies apart from Clone Power. Give a copy of the figures to Isabel Archer. She and I will analyse them on Friday next.

CLONE POWER

MEMORANDUM

To: George Shaw
From: Priscilla Khan
Subject: Reconditioned machine sales
Date: 24 June, 1994

I think you should talk to our dealers about our reconditioned machines. I think we have a problem with these machines/these dealers. Pete was talking to Irving Miller of the South Street shop, and Irving/Pete wasn't happy after the conversation. Irving said that the profit margin on a reconditioned machine was just too low compared to that of a new machine, and that such a/this situation just wasn't good enough. Irving's/He's the kind of person who doesn't know much about customer psychology, a fact which Pete hasn't yet understood.

What the dealers don't seem to understand is that our research shows that customers tend to buy the more expensive machines after they have become uncomfortable with the limitations of the reconditioned machines. This research was done specifically for our marketing department, so it's no wonder that the dealers don't understand it. Yet when I was in retailing, I/we/retail staff knew these things as a matter of course. The dealers say that customers won't lay out cash on more elaborate systems or even upgrade their reconditioned systems, but both of these things happen. I know both things happen.

Possible answers

INTERNAL MEMORANDUM

To: Irene Adler	Subject: R & D/ Team B
From: Satoshi Sakamoto	Date: 29 April, 1995

The Research and Development Department is giving us a hard time on gathering data from our experimental assembly team, Team B. Can you please intervene? Members of the department and their supervisor, Brian Maddox, think we've got it easy here, but that is not so. We're having trouble organising the data: we're collating data from more than one project, and so far they are proving to be contradictory. Brian doesn't seem to understand this, and isn't happy even when we give him these data. Statistics is what he majored in in his degree, but it's a pity he can't understand what these statistics are saying.

   We are also having trouble with the team, data or no data. The team agrees that efficiency has to be improved in all three areas, but it (or *such efficiency*, to avoid pronoun reference problems) is slow in happening. I've put a new member (Belinda Hawkins) on the team, and I hope that this makes a difference. Each of the members of the team has to accept his or her responsibility from now on. The typical team member has to see that pay and job security are what he or she chooses to make them. (Or — *All team members have to see that pay and security are what they choose to make them.*)

Suggested solution

JUGGERNAUT
MANUFACTURING, Inc

1000 Eastmore Road, Newtown 68113 Freedonia

Telephone (61.2) 419.6911 • Toll-free (61) 008.420.4322
• Facsimile (61.2) 419.6924 • Telex (61.2) 54437 JUGGER.

Dear Dr Jones:

Thank you for your letter of 16 June.

I was extremely impressed by the report comparing the test-bed performances of your AKJ-10 and the Visigoth brand B-6 machine we have been successfully using on our assembly lines. If your data is correct, then (use either *clearly* or *definitely*, but not both; use *I think it's clear* or *I think it's definite* if you wish to avoid disjuncts) (clearly) the AKJ-10 is (definitely) the better of the two machines. We may have a unique opportunity here to do business, but we will need to proceed carefully.

My opinion is that we need to test some innovations in this field really/quite/very quickly, so long as any fundamentals we seem to discover are not illusory/an illusion. Any facts that emerged from such a thorough procedure would provide (either *sufficient* or *enough*, but not both) sufficient/enough justification to continue to explore the infinite possibilities of the AKJ-10. I would argue that/I (would) think that any planning would then be based upon (either *such* or *whatever*, but not both) such/whatever valuable data that was gathered, and I hope/possibly there would never be a need/would be no need to return/to go back to the old technology/yesterday's technology.

I think it's interesting that/it's interesting that the (either *entire* or *whole*, but not both) entire/whole B-6 assembly line mechanism has been producing fewer errors in the past week, and if it continues to perform well, then my superiors would be less likely/less inclined to consider/to think about the (type of) perfection of your AKJ-10 when they can have an almost perfect alternative/option.

Please ring, and we'll continue to talk/will talk further about this.

Regards,

Irene Adler

Irene Adler.

Suggested answers

CLONE POWER

MEMORANDUM

To: Pete Roget
From: Priscilla Khan
Subject: Consumer Survey
Date: 14 November, 1995

I'm concerned about the results of our most recent consumer survey (although I wonder sometimes who the researchers get to respond to these surveys). The typical consumer/Typical consumers apparently sees/see Clone Power as being too up-market, although he or she/they still think our entry-level models are more realistically priced. He or she/they thinks/think our 786 model is currently too expensive, although he or she/they expect prices of this and similar models to fall as the newer super-chips become cheaper. If we lead the way to cut prices sooner rather than later, consumers will choose us rather than our competitors. Do some calculations on price margins, and present them at next Wednesday's meeting.

I have this morning faxed the data to Miles in Jakarta. He has left a phone message for me, in which he acknowledges most of the trends but asks if we can delay discussing them until he returns.

The truth is that consumers need to be able to walk in to one of our shops and buy a powerful computer that costs less than $1500. And let's not forget their other concerns — software and low-radiation screens. To benefit most from such data, we have to take surveys like this seriously.

CLONE POWER

Site 39, Rintrah Industrial Park, Claymore 23121 Freedonia

Telephone (61.5) 233.4352 • Facsimile (61.5) 233.4378

MEMORANDUM

To: Pete Roget
From: George Shaw
Subject: Juggernaut
Date: 12 June, 1995

We need to talk about the Juggernaut contract. Let's get together tomorrow at 3. Juggernaut's stalling on this makes you question whether we are ever going to close the deal. How long do they think we can wait? Their Director of Purchasing rang me today and said that they might take about 55 more printers if we can give 3 per cent more discount. Can we deliver that number within a week?

JUGGERNAUT
MANUFACTURING, Inc

1000 Eastmore Road, Newtown 68113 Freedonia

Telephone (61.2) 419.6911 • Toll-free (61) 008.420.4322
• Facsimile (61.2) 419.6924 • Telex (61.2) 54437 JUGGER.

Mr Prakesh Shastri,
Manager,
Acquisitions Division,
Hubris Macroengineering,
2056 Lagrange Grove,
Oldtown 68023

Dear Mr Shastri,

Thank you for your letter of 4 September. It was most informative.

Our area manager, Jerry Wintour, will contact you to give you details of our updated components range. While we want to do the best deal for you, you may have to keep in mind that all factories that have used our products before have priority when we are shipping new orders.

Nevertheless, once we have finished this week's shipping, our warehouse people will let me know what we have available in the way of P200s, P450s and T320s. I'm sure that we can do business.

Yours sincerely,

John Alden

John Alden

JUGGERNAUT
MANUFACTURING, Inc

1000 Eastmore Road, Newtown 68113 Freedonia

Telephone (61.2) 419.6911 • Toll-free (61) 008.420.4322
• Facsimile (61.2) 419.6924 • Telex (61.2) 54437 JUGGER.

Mr Brian Hanrahan,
Area Manager,
Juggernaut Manufacturing, Inc.
5 Proximity Drive,
Smallville 45603

Dear Brian: (or ,)

Thanks for your letter of the 16th.

As I see it, we can do one of three things: we can simply junk the ineffective computers, including their monitors, and get new ones; we can upgrade them, and hope that the upgrading will eliminate the problem areas; or we could simply keep them as a backup, and simply re-design people's work, so that they weren't so dependent on computerised systems. I don't think that the last alternative is feasible, and the second one is risky. The first alternative is the most expensive one; however, it may be the only one we've got.

Here at head office, we've been dealing with a number of suppliers lately, including Universal Technics, Clone Power and Micro Masters. Clone Power seems to be the best of this lot. Contact them and get a quote for replacement and upgrade, and then make your own decision. Spending in this area is always painful; it may be necessary, nevertheless, if we are to avoid further, greater expenditure required to clean up after disasters. As Max Kopraum in Accounts always says: 'There's nothing quite so expensive as something cheap.'

Let me know how it goes.

Yours sincerely,

Satoshi Sakamoto

Satoshi Sakamoto

JUGGERNAUT
MANUFACTURING, Inc

INTERNAL MEMORANDUM	
To: Ben Rawlinson	Subject: Front Street warehouse
From: Miles Standish	Date: 18 September, 1995

We're bursting at the seams, Ben, and we need some temporary accommodation quickly. Sixteen new staff are being taken on in Administration, and we can't fit them in on the sixth and seventh floors. We've also received a big government manufacturing contract that has to be met quickly. A temporary production line that could produce six kilos a day of P4's is required.

I want you to inspect the Front Street warehouse and see if it could be used for either area's needs. Administration staff will be appointed by September 29, the same day as we receive 24 new computers from our suppliers, Clone Power. Manufacturing would need to have new spaces at about the same time.

It's imperative we do this ASAP. Please check the warehouse's general environment (its walls, painting, etc.), damp, dust levels and power situation. Also, please determine how involved it will be to upgrade men's and women's toilets.

CLONE POWER

MEMORANDUM

To: Priscilla Khan
From: George Shaw
subject: new markets
Date: 4 August — 1994 or 4 August, 1994

I'm concerned that we're not getting to as many sectors of the market as we should be. I'm reasonably happy about our relationship with the corporate sector (although this ongoing Juggernaut problem shows that our discount structure isn't as well understood as it could be). I think we do have a problem with the general market of computer users (,) and I think we shouldn't neglect this much longer.

I find that customers who aren't very knowledgeable about computers in general don't know we exist, whereas customers who have proceeded beyond the basics are aware of us; what we need to do is to get to that market of beginners.

I want to set up a meeting about this and I'd like all the marketing group to be there; however, you may have some thoughts yourself about whether anyone else should be there. As I see it, we need to discuss three things: (1) who (or Who) is in this untapped market? (2) why (or Why) are our competitors' approaches to these customers working while ours aren't? (and) (3) what (or What) strategies can we develop for the next three years?

I'd like us to meet on the 26th at 2:00 p.m. There are numerous potential customers out there — (or :, or ;) let's get to them. (or !)

JUGGERNAUT

MANUFACTURING, Inc

INSPECTION REPORT	
To: Miles Standish	Subject: Front Street warehouse
From: Ben Rawlinson	Date: 30 September, 1995

As per your memo of 7 June, I have inspected this site to evaluate its utility for
(a) office clerical staff (using new PCs from Clone Power)
(b) manufacturing assembly (new P700 numerical controllers)

A. CLERICAL SITE
A.1. Environment
The environment is not very positive. The paint is peeling from the walls, and graffiti is everywhere.
The panes in the windows have been vandalised also.
A.2. Damp
Rising damp is in the floor, and also in the east wall.
A.3. Dust
The plaster ceilings are quite old, and create a major dust problem. This would be a particular problem for personal computers. (Marketing had a dust problem with their computer on the fourth floor last year — they lost two megabytes of data before we fixed the ceiling.)
A.4. Power
Electricity is not reliable, given current wiring. The baud rate of the machines would be affected.

B. MANUFACTURING SITE
B.1. Environment
Not a great problem for the assembly crews. They're not as fussy as the clerical staff, so that a less expensive paint job would be adequate.
B.2. Damp
Not a problem: the assembly machines have to sit on heavy rubber mats, and the machines put out a fair amount of heat anyway, which may reduce the damp.
B.3. Dust
A minor problem for the machines: an extraction blower could be fitted, and this would prove quite adequate (the machines have disposable filters anyway).
B.4. Power
A problem: machines would need three-phase power, although we may be able to run cables from the main factory.

COST ESTIMATES (approx. $)
Option A: $17 500 (painting, damp drying and drainage, new ceiling, rewiring)
Option B: $1 300 (assuming no three-phase power; if three-phase needed, add $9200)

RECOMMENDATION: Locate manufacturing here; look elsewhere for clerical

EXERCISE 12.1:

VOCABULARY

JUGGERNAUT
MANUFACTURING, Inc

INTERNAL MEMORANDUM	
To: Satoshi Sakamoto	Subject: Various
From: Irene Adler	Date: July 12, 1995

Sorry I didn't catch up with you before I left — will ring you from Jakarta.

Hubris Macroengineering want me to come to their board luncheon on the 25th — please contact them and say *it's OK*. I'm *loath* to *accept their* hospitality, but *they're* a big client, so what can I do?

I expect that Dan Steel will be there, so I will need a background paper done before I go. When I last spoke to him, he seemed *uninterested* in the project, so I will just have to try and show him why we are so enthusiastic. His sole *criterion* for decision-making seems to be short-term profit, which *irritates* me more than I can say.

Prakesh Shastri of their Acquisitions Division will also be there, and this *raises/prompts the question* of our new range of numerical controllers. Can you get me some data on discounts for our full range of numerical controllers? The last time we met, he spoke hopefully of the prospects for further development, and was *virtually/figuratively/ quotation marks* head over heels at the prospect of the C-9 being available for under $3000. He is aware of cost factors, but the principal *criteria* for purchase he would apply would be on-*site* reliability and service back-up. *Regardless* of Steel's demonstrated *ability* to put road-blocks in our way, we have to remember that *it's* Shastri we have to concentrate on, and so that data is vital. He will not have a chance to look at the data in detail *because* he is flying out to their Madras site next week.

EXERCISE 13.1:

PARAGRAPHS

JUGGERNAUT
MANUFACTURING, Inc

INTERNAL MEMORANDUM	
To: George Shaw	Subject: Your new computer and software
From: Roberta Adams	Date: 14 June, 1995

Sorry you couldn't get to the training session. Setting up the Clone Power 786 computer isn't all that difficult if you've set one up before. I seem to recall that you said you'd set up your son's basic computer. This advanced model is similar in some ways, dissimilar in others. If you feel unsure about doing it this way, wait until I come in tomorrow morning.

Firstly, check to see you've got everything. You should have five boxes, containing the computer itself, the monitor, the keyboard, the printer, and the bits and pieces (mouse, cables). There should also be two software packages. There should be a word processing package, and a spreadsheet package.

It's wise to start by clearing your desk. Put the software to one side for the moment, and then begin unpacking the hardware. Position the computer where you think you'll be most comfortable with it. Don't forget to leave room for the keyboard. Place the monitor on top of the computer. Place the printer where it's close enough to reach, but far enough so that it doesn't clutter your workspace.

Before going any further, please gather up the boxes and plastic packaging and put them on the trolley. We are trying to recycle this material. (The cellophane wrapping on the software can just go in the bin.)

Now you can start connecting things. Take the dark blue cable coming out of the monitor, and connect it to the vertical rectangular plug marked V at the back of the computer. Next, connect the printer cable (that's the large cream-coloured one) to the rectangular slots at the back of the printer and the back of the computer. The printer plug on the computer has a P in yellow ink near it. Once the printer is connected, connect the keyboard plug to the round plug at the back of the computer. Make sure you match up the little 'teeth' in the keyboard plug with the holes in the computer plug.

Now you can get some power. Plug in the power leads to the printer, screen and computer, and then plug the other ends of the leads into the special power board. This board is designed to prevent voltage variation problems. Plug in the board to a power point, turn it on, and then turn on the appliances. Turn on the printer, screen and computer. The on/off switches are clearly marked on all three. You should get a light on the printer, a light that flashes once on the computer, and you should then get a *Windows* graphic on your screen.

Once you have some picture on your screen, you should then be able to load your software. I know you've done workshops on both of those, so I don't expect you'll have any trouble.

Once these are loaded, simply load your files, and away you go.

Good luck with all of the above. If any of this doesn't work out, just drop everything (not literally, of course!), turn everything off, leave it where it is, and lock up the room as you go. I'll work with you on it tomorrow.

ENDNOTES

•   •   •   •   •   •   •   •   •   •

1. American usage is that both adjectives and adverbs *modify*, whereas British usage tends to be that adverbs *modify* but adjectives *qualify*. See, for example, Burton (1984:35).

2. For a more detailed treatment of the types of nouns, see, for example, Chalker (1984).

3. Adapted from Chalker (1984:25–35), Fowler & Aarons (1992:173). Thomas (1992:1), when classifying nouns, also includes 'action nouns', or verbal nouns or gerunds. These will be discussed in this book as non-finite verbs — see p. 36.

4. Action verbs are also known as *dynamic* verbs, and being verbs are also known as *stative* verbs.

5. Some writers prefer to describe words such as *my*, *every* and *this* as determiners rather than adjectives (and *mine*, *everyone* and *this* as determiners rather than pronouns). See, for example, Chalker (1984).

6. 'Emile Durkheim (1858–1917) who, with Max Weber, was one of the two founders of modern sociology, early abandoned his Jewish faith and lived out the rest of his life as a religious sceptic.' (Santamaria [1993:20]); 'He stood rigidly still while Tai got to his feet, and Hook's breath came out noisily, and each freckle stood ghastlily out against the dirty scared white of his face.' (Hammett [1975:99]).

7. Complications are irritating at this early stage of considering dictionary entries, but if you are interested enough to consult this note, you may be interested to observe that there are two major entries of *read*, i.e., *read*¹ and *read*². *Read*¹ is the big one. As we shall see when we consider irregular verbs (p. 33), *read* is an irregular verb — thus, for example, it does not form its past tense with a simple *-ed* suffix as would do a regular verb (for example, *type*: I type [present tense], I typed [past tense].) The past tense of *read* is thus shown separately — it is spelled the same, but pronounced differently (I read [pronounced *reed*] the paper [present tense]; I read [pronounced *red*] the paper yesterday. Dictionaries, of course, use proper phonetic script to show pronunciation).

   At the beginning of the *read*¹ entry, we see the abbreviation *v.*, meaning verb. The majority of the entry is then taken up with various transitive and intransitive meanings. Notice, however, that there is also an *n.* there — meaning, of course, a noun. Meanings thirty-two and thirty-three of the entry relate to noun meanings (a good *read*).

Read^2 is an adjectival meaning (a widely *read* person). This adjectival meaning, as the note indicates, is properly the past participle form of *read*^{1}.

Don't worry about all this jargon: by the time you have considered the two other dictionary entries in this book (p. 41, p. 133), entries like that for *read* should appear to be a lot less complex and daunting.

8. *Should/would, shall/will*: Burton (1984:134); American Heritage Dictionary (1992:1657, 1670–71). Note also Fowler's lukewarm defence of the traditional model (Fowler [1990:548–551]), and Gowers' a-bit-both-ways treatment, including the anecdote about the drowning Scotsman: 'But the idiom of the Celts is different. They have never recognised "I shall go." For them "I will go" is the plain future. The story is a very old one of the drowning Scot who was misunderstood by English onlookers and left to his fate because he cried, "I will drown and nobody shall save me".' (Gowers [1987:141]).

9. Note that some writers prefer to refer to perfect and progressive tenses as aspects or forms. Note the differing treatments, for example, of Fowler & Aarons (1992), Troyka (1993), Burton (1982) and Quirk & Greenbaum (1973).

10. Note, for example, Burton (1984:134): 'Those lingering uses of a signalled subjunctive mood are themselves disappearing from modern English, and "mood" as a whole, is a concept of little practical significance to users of the English language.' Note also Gowers (1986:139): 'It is remarkable — for it seems contrary to the whole history of the development of the language — that under the influence of American English the use of the subjunctive is creeping back into British English.'

11. Johnston (1991:65)

12. Note Tichy's remarks about the evasive passive voice:

' "Always use the passive voice" is a prescription so frequently pressed on writers of informational prose that it has proved to be one of the most harmful fallacies, if not the most harmful. Frequently enunciated by a person in a position superior to a writer's, the fallacy bears the heavy weight of law. This erroneous advice may confront an engineer or scientist first in graduate school. There professors may insist that students write as the professors do, in the passive voice, in order to appear scholarly, to show objectivity, to acquire a style like that of journal articles, or — more brutally — to make papers acceptable. In business and industry some supervisors have discovered the use of the passive to evade responsibility and therefore use it as ruthlessly as politicians do . . .

'Readers of minutes written in the evasive passive often find themselves sounding like hoot owls as they scream, "Who? Who? Whoooo?" to statements like

The cost of the TV program was estimated incorrectly.

A letter to the FDA will be written.

A report on these dyes will be submitted.

It was said that the ruling will be ignored.

A suggestion was made that marketing be postponed two months.

It was reported that the new package has been well received.

'In such writing all agents are anonymous and many statements are ambiguous. Helpful and useful information is omitted. Nobody is responsible for anything.

'For a whole year an apocryphal head of a college department evaded responsibility by writing sentences like the following:

The new curriculum has been approved.

The two suggested promotions from assistant to associate professor have not been approved.

Budget allotments for travel have been reduced by twenty per cent.

An annual increase of $2500 for the head of the department has been recommended.

'Nobody knew it was this worm who had approved and not approved, had reduced and recommended. But at the end of the year his department discovered the evader behind the passive voice, and in the unmistakable active voice the members demanded his resignation.' (Tichy [1988:264, 266-267]).

Note also the use of the evasive passive in politics:

'There is a less honorable use of the passive however, one politicians have a tendency to rely on — that is, to evade responsibility. William Safire in his *New York Times* column, "On Language", comments on this predilection, focusing on former White House chief-of-staff John Sununu, who, when asked at a press conference about the use of government funds for personal expenses, replied, "Obviously, some mistakes were made."

'Safire notes that "The passive voice acknowledges the errors, but it avoids the blame entirely ... When deniability is impossible, dissociation is the way, and the (passive voice) allows the actor to separate himself from the act." ' (Cooper & Patton [1993:203-204]).

13. Garner (1989:182)

14. Formally, there are at least ten adverbial clauses, that is, clauses of time (which answer the question when?), place (where?), manner (how?), reason or cause (why?), purpose (for what purpose?), result or consequence (with what result?), condition (under what condition(s)?), concession (even though what?), comparison (compared with what?), and degree or extent (to what degree?). See Burton (1984), Ehrlich (1992).

15. Modifies the adverb, or the verb? For some answers to this question, see Burton (1984:97).

16. 'A complex sentence in which the noun clause is the subject provides an exception to the rule that a main clause makes sense on its own. Indeed, it is misleading to describe such sentences as having a main clause, for neither clause makes sense without the other ...' (Burton, 1984:101).

17. Some are more charitable towards expletives: 'Because they postpone the subject, expletive constructions slow the pace of a sentence and can be useful for gaining the reader's attention. They announce "Get ready. Something is coming. Don't miss it." Expletives can provide effective sentence variety, but they can also create unnecessary clutter in a sentence and so should be used thoughtfully.' (Leggett, Mead & Kramer [1991:10])

18. See, for example, Burton (1984). Heffernan & Lincoln (1990) also consider the reflexive/emphatic case — myself, himself, themselves. etc.

19. Adapted from Troyka (1993:210), Fowler & Aarons (1992:213), and Leggett, Mead & Kramer (1991:23).

20. Be careful how you use pronouns, because you might end up using an adjective (or adverb) instead. A pronoun stands in place of a noun or pronoun, an adjective modifies a noun or pronoun, while an adverb modifies a verb, adjective or adverb. *Each*, for example, can be all three: *Each* of the boys sang (pronoun); *Each* boy sang (adjective); He gave the boys ten cents *each* (adverb). Remember: the part of speech of a word in a sentence is determined by the function of that word in a sentence. See the section on pronouns and adjectives, p. 20.

21. Note that some pronouns — *my, your, his*, etc. — can be adjectives in some sentences. See discussion of adjectives versus pronouns, p. 20.

22. Quoted in Crystal (1985:96)

23. See, for example, Burchfield (1991), Bryson (1991), Crystal (1985), Spears (1991). The editors of the *American Heritage Dictionary* refer controversial words to a usage panel of over 100 Americans, eminent in various fields. In the first edition of the dictionary (1969), 44 per cent of the panel accepted the newer usage of *hopefully*, but by the third edition (1992), this had declined to 27 per cent — a fact which annoyed the editors in their reporting of the findings. Thus, even in a dictionary, a usage panel can be prescriptivist while the editors are descriptivist. (*American Heritage Dictionary* [1992: 870–871])

24. Tichy (1988:266)

25. Alex Buzo gives his (humorous) decodings of some disjuncts:
    Hopefully — Forget it.
    Arguably — I haven't done my research.
    Paul Dickson has done some similar decoding of disjuncts beloved of journalists:
    Presumably — Code word telling the reader that the writer is about to take a wild-assed guess.
    Reportedly — This means we have no idea if this is so, but it sounds good.
    (Buzo [1981], Dickson [1992])

26. Example from Gowers (1987:233)

27. See, for example, Poyatos (1983).

28. The treatment of punctuation here is extensive, but not exhaustive. For more detailed treatments, see Troyka (1993), (Shaw 1993b), Fowler & Aarons (1992), Ehrlich (1992), Thomas (1992), and Markgraf (1979).

29. 'An instruction book called "Pre-aircrew English", supplied during the (Second World War) to airmen in training in a Commonwealth country, contained an encouragement to its readers to "smarten up their English". This ended:

    Pilots, whose minds are dull, do not usually live long.

    The commas convert a truism into an insult.'
    (Gower [1987:159]).

30. British and American usage varies here: what Americans call *parentheses*, the British call *brackets*, and what Americans call *brackets*, the British call *square brackets*. American usage is followed here. Note also that parenthesis is a generic term that simply means something that is inserted — a digression, an explanation, or other remark — in a sentence. Such an insertion can be punctuated with parentheses/brackets, brackets/square brackets, dashes, or commas. Claims that each of these types of parentheses have many unique and technically precise applications, which set them fundamentally apart from other types of parenthetical punctuation, should be taken with a grain of salt.

31. Crystal (1988:214)

32. 'Indo-European Roots', *American Heritage Dictionary* (1992:2131)

33. *American Heritage Dictionary* (1992:2024)

34. See Bryson (1990), Chapter 4, and McCrum, Cran & McNeil (1987), Chapter 2.

35. McCrum, Cran & McNeil (1987:75). French of course was derived from Latin.

36. 'The statistics of English are astonishing. Of all the world's languages (which now number some 2700), it is arguably the richest in vocabulary. The compendious *Oxford English Dictionary* lists about 500 000 words; and a further half-million technical and scientific terms remain uncatalogued. According to traditional estimates, neighbouring German has a vocabulary of about 185 000 words and French fewer than 100 000, including such Franglais as *le snacquebarre* and *le hit parade*.' (McCrum, Cran & McNeil, 1987:19)

37. Crystal (1988:214)

38. See, for example, McCrum, Cran & McNeil (1987), McArthur (1992), Bryson (1991).

39. See Fowler (1990:22–25).

40. British use of the *-ise* suffix is by no means universal: Fowler notes that there are many authentic usages of the Greek and Latin *-ize* in preference to the French *-ise* (Fowler 1990:314).

41. *American Heritage Dictionary* (1992:2120). Note the etymological abbreviations in the two other dictionary entries reproduced in *Writing Skills*:
   - *read* (*Macquarie Dictionary*), p. 26: ME = Middle English; OE = Old English; D = Dutch; G = German; Icel. = Icelandic.
   - *speak* (*New Shorter Oxford Dictionary*) p. 41: OE = Old English; ME = Middle English; OFris = Old Frisian; OS = Old Saxon; OHG = Old High German; Du = Dutch; G = German; WGmc = West Germanic; ON = Old Norse.

   The verb *type* is formed from the noun form of the same word, which is not reproduced here. The word derives from the Latin *typus*, which in turn is derived from the Greek *tupos* (blow, impression, image, figure).
42. Some of these definitions are taken or adapted from Roberts (1988); Strunk & White (1979); Shaw (1975); Urdang (1992); Reader's Digest (1992); *American Heritage Dictionary* (Third Edition) (1992); *Oxford Advanced Learner's Dictionary of Current English* (Third Edition) (1978).
43. Examples and analysis of begging the question taken from Cooper & Patton (1993:159–160).

REFERENCE LIST

• • • • • • • • •

American Heritage Dictionary of the English Language, The (1992) (Third Edition) (Boston, MA: Houghton Mifflin)

Barzun, Jacques (1992) 'What If?: English versus German and French', in Gross, John (ed.) *The Oxford Book of Essays* (Oxford: Oxford University Press)

Beazley, Malcolm and Marr, Grahame (1992) *The Writers' Handbook* (Albert Park, Victoria: Phoenix Education)

Booher, Diane (1988) *Good Grief, Good Grammar: The Business Person's Guide to Grammar and Usage* (New York: Ballantine Books)

Brittain, Robert (1982) *A Pocket Guide to Correct Punctuation* (Woodbury, New York: Barron's Educational Series)

Brock, Susan L. (1988) *Better Business Writing* (Revised Edition) (Los Altos, California: Crisp Publications, Inc.)

Bryson, Bill (1991) *Mother Tongue: the English Language* (Harmondsworth, Middlesex: Penguin)

Bryson, Bill (1984) *The Penguin Dictionary of Troublesome Words* (Harmondsworth, Middlesex: Penguin)

Burchfield, Robert (1992) *Points of View: Aspects of Present-Day English* (Oxford: Oxford University Press)

Burchfield, Robert (1987) *The English Language* (Oxford: Oxford University Press)

Burton, S. H. (1984) *Mastering English Grammar* (London/Basingstoke: Macmillan Education)

Buzo, Alex (1981) *Meet the New Class* (Sydney: Angus & Roberston)

Callihan, E. L. (1979) *Grammar for Journalists* (Radnor, Pennsylvania: Chilton Book Company)

Carmichael, Claire (1986) *English: the Essentials* (Melbourne: Longman Cheshire)

Chalker, Sylvia (1984) *Current English Grammar* (London/Basingstoke: Macmillan)

Chicago Manual of Style, The (Thirteenth Edition) (1982) (Chicago, Ill.: University of Chicago Press)

Claiborne, Robert (1990) *The Life and Times of the English Language: the History of our Marvellous Native Tongue* (London: Bloomsbury)

Clark, John W. (1967) *Early English: An Introduction to Old And Middle English* (Revised Edition) (London: Andre Deutsch)

Cooper, Sheila and Patton, Rosemary (1993) *Ergo: Thinking Critically and Writing Logically* (New York: HarperCollins)

Corish, R. C. and Carter, S. (1992) *Practical English* (Third Edition) (South Melbourne: Pitman)

Crystal, David (1985) *Who Cares about English Usage?* (Harmondsworth, Middlesex: Penguin)

Crystal, David (1988a) *The English Language* (Harmondsworth, Middlesex: Penguin)

Crystal, David (1988b) (ed.) *The Cambridge Encyclopedia of Language* (Cambridge: Cambridge University Press)

D'Eloia, Sarah (1987) 'The Uses — and Limits — of Grammar', in Enos, Theresa (ed.) *A Sourcebook for Basic Writing Teachers* (New York: Random)

Dickson, Paul (1981) *The Official Explanations* (London: Arrow Books)

Dickson, Paul (1992) *Dickson's Word Treasury: A Connoisseur's Collection of Old and New, Weird and Wonderful, Useful and Outlandish Words* (New York: John Wiley & Sons)

Eagleson, Robert D. (1990) *Writing in Plain English* (Canberra: Australian Government Publishing Service)

Ehrlich, Eugene and Murphy, Daniel (1991) *Schaum's Outline of English Grammar* (Second Edition) (New York: McGraw-Hill)

Ehrlich, Eugene (1992) *Schaum's Outline of Theory and Problems of Punctuation, Capitalisation, and Spelling* (Second Edition) (New York: McGraw-Hill)

Eunson, Baden (1990) 'Semantics of the Anti-Creed: The Use of "Hopefully" ', *Sunday Herald*, March 11

Fawcett, Susan and Sandberg, Alvin (1990) *Business English: Skills for Success* (Boston: Houghton Mifflin)

Fowler, H. W. (1990) *A Dictionary of Modern English Usage* (Second Edition. Revised by Sir Ernest Gowers) (London/Oxford: Book Club Associates/Oxford University Press)

Fowler, H. Ramsey and Aaron, Jane E. (1992) *The Little, Brown Handbook* (Fifth Edition) (New York: HarperCollins)

Freeborn, Dennis (1987) *A Course Book in English Grammar* (London/Basingstoke: Macmillan)

Furness, Edna L. (1990) *Guide to Better English Spelling* (Lincolnwood, Illinois: National Textbook Company)

Garner, Mark (1989) *Grammar: Warts and All* (Melbourne: River Seine Press)

Gee, Robyn and Watson, Carol (1990) *The Usborne Book of Better English* (Saffron Hill, London: Usborne)

Gilbert, Marilyn B. (1983) *Clear Writing: A Business Guide* (New York: John Wiley & Sons)

Gordon, Karen Elizabeth (1983) *The Well-Tempered Sentence: A Punctuation Handbook for the Innocent, the Eager and the Doomed* (New Haven and New York: Ticknor and Fields)

Gordon, Karen Elizabeth (1984) *The Transitive Vampire: A Handbook of Grammar for the Innocent, The Eager and the Doomed* (New York: Times Books)

Gowers, Sir Ernest (1987) *The Complete Plain Words* (Harmondsworth, Middlesex: Penguin)

Greenbaum, Sydney and Whitcut, Janet (1988) *Longman Guide to English Usage* (London: Longman)

Hall, Nick and Shepheard, John (1991) *The Anti-Grammar Grammar Book* (London: Longman)

Hammett, Dashiell (1984) 'The House in Turk Street', in *The Continental Op* (London: Pan Books)

Heaton, J. B. and Turton, N. D. (1990) *Longman Dictionary of Common Errors* (London: Longman)

Heffernan, James A. W. and Lincoln, John E. (1990) *Writing: A College Workbook* (Third Edition) (New York: W. W. Norton & Company)

Hopper, Vincent, Gale, Cedric, Foote, Ronald C., and Griffith, Benjamin W. (1984) *A Pocket Guide to Correct Grammar* (New York: Barron's Educational Series)

Hopper, Vincent F. and Gale, Cedric (1991) *Essentials of Writing* (Fourth Edition: Revised by Griffith, Benjamin W. Jr.) (New York: Barron's Educational Series, Inc.)

Howard, Peter (1986) *Mistakes to Avoid in English* (Melbourne: Longman Cheshire)

Huddleston, Rodney (1988) *English Grammar: An Outline* (Cambridge: Cambridge University Press)

Hudson, Kenneth (1977) *The Dictionary of Diseased English* (London & Basingstoke: Macmillan)

Johnson, Edward D. (1991) *The Handbook of Good English* (New York: Washington Square Press/Pocket Books)

Leech, Geoffrey, Deuchar, Margaret and Hoogenraad, Robert (1982) *English Grammar for Today: A New Introduction* (London/Basingstoke: Macmillan)

Leggett, Glen, Mead, C. David and Kramer, Melinda G. (1991) *Prentice-Hall Handbook for Writers* (Eleventh Edition) (Englewood Cliffs, New Jersey: Prentice-Hall)

Little, Greta D. (1986) 'The Ambivalent Apostrophe', *English Today*, October

Longman Dictionary of English Language and Culture (1993) (London: Longman)

Markgraf, Carl (1979) *Punctuation* (New York: John Wiley & Sons)

McArthur, Tom (1992) *Oxford Companion to the English Language* (Oxford: Oxford University Press)

McCrum, Robert, Cran, William and MacNeil, Robert (1987) *The Story of English* (London: Faber)

Nesfield, J. C. and Wood, F. T. (1964) *Manual of English Grammar and Composition* (London/Basingstoke: Macmillan)

Neuberger, Thomas R. (1989) *Foundation: Building Sentence Skills* (Boston: Houghton Mifflin)

Newby, Michael (1987) *The Structure of English: A Handbook of English Grammar* (Cambridge: Cambridge University Press)

Osburn, Patricia (1989) *How Grammar Works: A Self-Teaching Guide* (New York: John Wiley & Sons)

Oxford English Dictionary (Second Edition) (Twenty Volumes) (1989) (Oxford: Oxford University Press)

Oxford Advanced Learner's Dictionary of Current English (Third Edition) (1978) (Oxford: Oxford University Press)

Partridge, Eric (1973) *Usage and Abusage* (Harmondsworth, Middlesex: Penguin)

Perrin, Robert (1990) *The Beacon Handbook* (Second Edition) (Boston: Houghton Mifflin)

Poyatos, Fernando (1983) 'Punctuation as Nonverbal Communication: Toward a Revision of the System', in *New Perspectives in Nonverbal Communication* (Oxford: Pergamon)

Quirk, Randolph and Greenbaum, Sidney (1973) *A University Grammar of English* (Harlow, Essex: Longman)

Reader's Digest Services (1992) *How to Write and Speak Better* (Second Edition) (Sydney: Reader's Digest)

Reed, Bill and Nolan, Sharon (1993) *Business English Teacher's Resourcebook* (London: Longman)

Roberts, Philip Davies (1988) *Plain English: A User's Guide* (Harmondsworth, Middlesex: Penguin)

Safire, William (1993) *Good Advice on Writing* (Sydney: Simon & Schuster)

Santamaria, B. A. (1993) 'Families, not Fantasies, are our Future', The *Weekend Australian*, January 2–3. p. 20

Schoenheimer, Henry P. (1976) *Expressive English: A Handbook for Senior Students* (Melbourne: Longman Cheshire)

Shaw, Harry (1975) *Dictionary of Problem Words and Expressions* (New York: Washington Square)

Shaw, Harry (1993a) *Errors in English and Ways to Correct Them* (Fourth Edition) (New York: HarperCollins)

Shaw, Harry (1993b) *Punctuate it Right!* (Second Edition) (New York: HarperCollins)

Shaw, Harry (1993c) *Spell it Right!* (Fourth Edition) (New York: HarperCollins)

Snodgrass, Gladys (1992) *English at Work* (Third Edition) (South Melbourne: Pitman)

Spears, Richard C. (1991) *NTC's Dictionary of Grammar Terminology* (Lincolnwood, Illinois: National Textbook Company)

Strunk, William, Jr., and White, E. B. (1979) *The Elements of Style* (Third Edition) (New York: Macmillan)

Strutt, Peter (1993) *Longman Business English Usage* (London: Longman)

Swan, Michael (1991) *Practical English Usage* (Revised Edition) (Oxford: Oxford University Press)

Swenson, Jack (1991) *The Building Blocks of Business Writing: The Foundation of Writing Skills* (Los Altos, California: Crisp Publications, Inc.)

Swenson, Jack (1988) *Writing Fitness: Practical Exercises for Better Business Writing* (Los Altos, California: Crisp Publications, Inc.)

Thomas, Susan G, (1992) *Grammar and Punctuation Essentials for Business Communication* (Cincinnati, Ohio, South-Western Publishing)

Tichy, H. J., with Fourdrinier, Sylvia (1988) *Effective Writing for Engineers, Managers, Scientists* (Second Edition) (New York: John Wiley & Sons)

Troyka, Lyn Quitman (1993) *Simon and Schuster Handbook for Writers* (Third Edition) (Englewood Cliffs: Prentice-Hall)

Trudgill, Peter and Hannah, Jean (1985) *International English: A Guide to Varieties of Standard English* (Second Edition) (London: Edward Arnold)

Urdang, Laurence (1992) *Dictionary of Differences* (London: Bloomsbury)

Vermes, Jean C. (1991) *Secretary's Guide to Modern English Usage* (Second Edition: Revised by Barnum, Carol M.) (Englewood Cliffs, New Jersey: Prentice-Hall)

Waterhouse, Keith (1991) *English Our English (And How to Sing It)* (London: Viking/Penguin)

Watkins, Floyd C. and Dillingham, William B. (1989) *Practical English Handbook* (Eighth Edition) (Boston: Houghton Mifflin)

Webster's Dictionary of English Usage (1989) (Springfield, MA: Merriam-Webster)

World Book of Word Power, The, Vol 1 (Language) and Vol 2 (Writing and Speaking) (1991) (Chicago: World Book, Inc.)